200 Best
Panini
Recipes

Tiffany Collins

Robert
ROSE

For complete cataloguing information, see page 250.

Disclaimer
The recipes in this book have been carefully tested by our kitchen and our tasters. To the best of our knowledge, they are safe and nutritious for ordinary use and users. For those people with food or other allergies, or who have special food requirements or health issues, please read the suggested contents of each recipe carefully and determine whether or not they may create a problem for you. All recipes are used at the risk of the consumer. Consumers should always consult their panini grill manufacturer's manual for recommended procedures and cooking times.

We cannot be responsible for any hazards, loss or damage that may occur as a result of any recipe use.

For those with special needs, allergies, requirements or health problems, in the event of any doubt, please contact your medical adviser prior to the use of any recipe.

Design and Production: Daniella Zanchetta/PageWave Graphics Inc.
Editor: Sue Sumeraj
Recipe Tester: Jennifer MacKenzie
Proofreader: Sheila Wawanash
Indexer: Belle Wong
Photography: Colin Erricson
Food Styling: Kathryn Robertson and Ross Crawford
Prop Styling: Charlene Erricson

Cover image: Grilled Chicken, Spinach, Red Pepper and Pepper Jack Panini (page 93)

We acknowledge the financial support of the Government of Canada through the Book Publishing Industry Development Program (BPIDP) for our publishing activities.

Published by Robert Rose Inc.
120 Eglinton Avenue East, Suite 800, Toronto, Ontario, Canada M4P 1E2
Tel: (416) 322-6552 Fax: (416) 322-6936
www.robertrose.ca

Printed and bound in Canada

11 12 13 14 MP 16 15 14 13 12

In loving memory of my mother, Fay Tacker, who was and continues to be a culinary inspiration in so many ways. And to Kennedy, my precious daughter, who gives me endless joy, love and happiness.

Contents

Acknowledgments

I CANNOT THANK MY FRIENDS and family enough for their love and support while I was writing this book. I am especially thankful to my agent, Lisa Ekus-Saffer, who believed in me and opened my eyes to so many opportunities. Lisa continues to help me open doors I thought were locked. Thank you to Sarah Baurle with the Lisa Ekus Group for trusting her instinct and my talent. Thank you to Bob Dees, my publisher, for trusting this first-time author and to Sue Sumeraj, my editor, for her patient guidance throughout the writing and editing process. Thanks also to Daniella Zanchetta of PageWave Graphics for her beautiful design, and to the photography team — Colin Erricson, Kathryn Robertson and Charlene Erricson — for their gorgeous photographs.

Many of my friends invested their time to help me with this project. My dear friend Ellen Harrison and her parents, John and Catherine Sullivan, sat with me and brainstormed hundreds of recipe titles and flavor combinations over endless glasses of wine. Ellen tested and double-tested, purchased groceries and helped me decide which panini makers just didn't make the cut.

My friends at the Texas Beef Council, Lorill Sleeper, Jill Hodgkins, Michele Blank, Linda Bebee, Jennifer Matison and Pam Wortham, gave me many panini ideas and lots of support.

My dear friend Meg Plotsky made hundreds of phone calls to lend me endless support and love. My friend and workout partner Marcia Smith gave me many suggestions for healthy choices. Larry Russo provided inspiration from his Italian heritage. Tina and Jordan Manson sent countless emails suggesting flavor combinations that kids would enjoy. Whenever I appeared as a guest on a television show, my dear friend and sister-in-law Jody Tacker insisted that her medical practice keep the television tuned to that channel. Thanks for helping me develop a fan base.

Thanks also to Bobby Collins, my former husband and friend, for believing in me and giving me your support. To my daddy, John Tacker, for helping mold me into the person I am today and encouraging me to strive to be the best person I can be. We missed having Mom during this process, but were able to reminisce about her fabulous meals and use her recipes as inspiration.

To Kennedy, my wonderful little girl, for volunteering countless opinions — which were certainly honest, to say the least! Thank you for tasting so many panini recipes and for gently letting me know that mac and cheese would be just fine for dinner, and I didn't have to go to the trouble of making you another panini.

To my siblings, Jill and Bud: we have shared many meals filled with laughter and love. What an amazing dining experience each has been. To Roger and Carol Johnson, who have helped me appreciate the value of taking risks and trusting.

And finally, to Tim Johnson, TJ, a wonderful man to whom I owe so much. You have grown to love, understand and support me in ways I never thought possible. From the conception of this book, you were there to say, "You *can* do this, Tif, and you *will* do this." You stood by my side, tasting recipes, and stayed clear when things were a bit tough. You have tasted bad panini and good panini and kept coming back for more, thank goodness. I am also grateful that your beautiful children, Derek, Emmy and Griffin, shared this amazing experience.

Introduction

Whe I WAS ASKED to write *200 Best Panini Recipes*, my initial reaction was, You better know I will! Then I thought, Are there really 200 panini recipes?

But just as my mom was, I am the master of sandwiches. I have been told I make the best sandwiches, and I think this is because I believe sandwich ingredients have zero limitations. And what is a panini but a pressed, grilled sandwich? When I looked at it that way, I knew I could create 200 *plus*.

The potential ingredient lineups for sandwiches are endless, as are the combinations of flavors, both traditional and unusual. And you can take almost any sandwich and turn it into a panini, with a bit of landscaping. You know, to keep the ingredients from oozing out too much. Once you step outside of the panini "box," you'll find that there are a million irresistible possibilities.

In this book, I've included many of my favorite sandwiches, such as Turkey Panini with Cranberry Chutney and Sunflower Seeds (page 110), Beef and Brie Panini (page 127) and Shrimp Club Panini (page 80). I put my own spin on some traditional sandwich recipes, such as the Classic Reuben Panini (page 135), the Monte Cristo Panini (page 143) and the Philly Chicken Panini (page 182). I figured out ways to reinvent other recipes I enjoy as delicious panini, as with the Chicken Caesar Panini (page 92), the Lobster Fontina Panini (page 84) and my signature sandwich, The Tiffany (page 166), which incorporates my favorite pizza toppings. I polled my friends and family to learn what flavor combinations they enjoy and turned those ingredients into panini, such as Marcia's Tuna and Swiss Panini (page 62) and the Open-Face Hawaiian Melt (page 218), my daughter's favorite treat. And I experimented to create brand-new flavor combinations that exceeded even my own expectations, such as Smashed White Bean, Avocado and Bacon Panini (page 158), Sardine and Balsamic Tomato Panini (page 64) and Mixed Berry and Mascarpone Panini with Toasted Almonds (page 227).

But before we get to my 200 recipes, let's talk about your equipment and ingredient options.

Equipment

YOU HAVE A FEW different options when it comes to choosing a panini grill, each with its own pluses and minuses.

Panini Pan and Press

This product is a two-piece panini grill, usually consisting of a nonstick pan that offers even heat retention and a heavy-duty press with a loop handle that provides added pressure on top, giving the tops of sandwiches grill marks. These grills are usually made of cast iron, with a porcelain enamel interior and exterior, and are available in many colors.

The nonstick pan is also useful as a multipurpose pan, as it is able to go from stovetop to oven, and is oven-safe up to 500°F (260°C). The nonstick surface cleans easily, though washing by hand is usually recommended.

This type of panini grill is great for grilling meats, vegetables and fruits, as the ridged bottom brings the pleasure of outdoor grilling indoors, with authentic grill marks for steaks, chops and burgers, not to mention panini.

Panini Maker

Electric panini makers can be found at superstores, at specialty kitchen shops and even at higher-end grocery stores, at prices ranging from $35 to $130 plus. Specialty brands at gourmet kitchen stores are pricier. I didn't mind paying a bit more, as the more expensive brands have added features for different cooking methods and menu items. Panini makers are perfect for grilling sandwiches, and some models also allow you to grill meats, vegetables and fruits.

> ### Be Careful!
> Most panini makers get *very* hot on the outer surface. I always use a potholder when I open and close the grill.

Electric Griddle

The surface area of an electric griddle means several sandwiches can be grilled at one time. However, if you use a griddle, you will need a pressing device to press the sandwich into a true panini. I used a clean brick wrapped with heavy-duty foil or my grandmother's cast-iron skillet, which I was lucky enough to inherit. The obvious drawback is that several bricks, or a couple of skillets, are needed; it *could* work, but it doesn't seem like the most logical option. Therefore, an electric griddle would not be my choice for panini grilling, even if the upside is volume.

Features to look for in a panini maker

- Many panini makers offer a retro look, with stainless-steel housing. These look nice on countertops, and as I always say, if it's stored away in a box, chances are you won't use it.

- A floating top plate can be adjusted so that it is level, rather than at an angle, when shut. This feature is useful when your panini contains ingredients that might ooze out if the sandwich was pressed at an angle.

- Pop-out plates are easy to remove and dishwasher-safe. Some models come with two types of plates — grill plates and flat griddle plates — allowing you to choose between grilling and toasting. (*One note of caution:* I used the dishwasher to clean grill plates and ended up damaging them. So even if your grill plates claim to be dishwasher-safe, I'd wash them by hand to be on the safe side.)

- Some models offer a larger surface area than others. However, most of the recipes in this book are for 2 sandwiches, which will fit comfortably in the regular-sized panini makers.

- Indicator lights, adjustable temperature controls, heat-resistant handles and hidden cord storage are all great features.

- Plastic scrapers will help you scrape up all the yummy cheese that inevitably melts onto the plates. If your panini maker doesn't come with one, and is nonstick, make sure to use a plastic or wood spatula to scrape the plates, as metal will damage the nonstick surface.

- Many grill plates are designed to drain grease away from food, for much healthier cooking. Drip cups are a valuable feature if you intend to use your panini maker to grill meats or juicy veggies in addition to making panini.

- An upright storage design allows you to stow your panini maker in more compact spaces.

Ingredients

ONCE YOU GET GOING on making panini, you will find that there are really many more than 200 recipes in this book. That's because every recipe has an unlimited number of potential variations. In many recipes, I've suggested variations, but I'm sure you will think of others on your own. Sandwiches are meant to be easy and fun, so experiment as much as you like and adjust the ingredients to your own taste. Of course, after a long day, when you're just not up to thinking, rely on me — I've put together 200 fantastic taste combinations for you.

When you're creating your own panini recipes, there's one important guideline to keep in mind: a good sandwich incorporates a variety of textures, from crusty bread to creamy melted cheese, and from tender sliced meat to crisp, crunchy fruits and veggies.

Breads

In my opinion, the bread is the most important ingredient when it comes to panini — it is, after all, the foundation on which the sandwich is built. And your bread options are limitless: you can use any freshly baked bread of your choice. In my recipes, I use many different types of bread, each with its own personality.

For my first homemade panini, I used the presliced, packaged wheat bread found in the grocery store. This type of bread is very soft, so if you press down on the top plate of your panini maker, you end up with a panini you can practically slide under a door. For my second panini, I used the same bread but did not force down the top plate. When I use this type of bread to make PB&J and Banana Panini (page 210) for my daughter, I hold the top plate so that it barely touches the top bread slice, which is perfect! I prefer this technique to grilling sandwiches in a pan, as there is no turning needed.

Ciabatta, the bread traditionally used for panini recipes, is a much denser, harder bread. Recipes often tell you to slice off the domed top of the ciabatta roll; my way of thinking is, make it the way *you* like it or the way the person eating it likes it. Focaccia, another dense bread, often comes in wonderful flavors that can be used to augment or complement the ingredients inside. Try focaccia flavored with olives or sun-dried tomatoes, for example, with the Mediterranean Gobbler (page 114).

Submarine, hoagie and French rolls will house a large amount of ingredients. My Spicy Barbecue Steak Panini with Crispy Onions (page 190) requires a big bite — not that that is a bad thing!

If you use a softer bread, such as buttery croissants, be careful not to press hard, or you will have croissant pancakes! I don't use croissants often in my recipes, but I love Salami and Fontina Croissants (page 168).

Each of my recipes specifies a bread to use, but these are not set in stone. In almost every case, different types of bread will work well. Experiment to find the combinations you like best.

Cheeses

Just about any cheese will work in a panini recipe — soft, hard, semi-hard, you name it. The cheese can be sliced, shredded, grated, crumbled or spread, depending on the type of cheese you use and how much you want it to melt while it is grilling. Just keep an eye on it to make sure it doesn't melt right out of its crusty foundation onto the grill! You can use a single type of cheese, or a mix of two or more cheeses for a delightful combination of flavors.

Meats and Fish

When you're thinking of meats to put in your sandwiches, the first thing that comes to mind is probably sliced deli meats or canned fish. And these, of course, are wonderful for their ease of preparation and flavor. But you can also make fabulous panini from meats and fish you've grilled or roasted yourself, or from leftovers. In the recipes in this book, you will find panini made with a wide array of meats and meat alternatives: beef, poultry, pork, specialty meats, fish, seafood, beans and tofu.

Fruits and Veggies

The crunch of fresh cucumber, the juiciness of a summer heirloom tomato, the sweet bite of red onion, the heat of jalapeño peppers, the unique texture of alfalfa sprouts — all lend amazing dimension and flavor to panini. You're probably used to putting sliced veggies in your sandwiches, but don't forget about fruit! Ripe, juicy pears are the star in Spinach, Pear and Walnut Panini with Feta (page 37), and the apple steals the spotlight with its burst of flavor in Apple, Cheddar and Bacon Bagels (page 20). Sliced fruit also makes scrumptious dessert panini.

Condiments

There are so many options when it comes to condiments for panini recipes. Mayonnaise, mustard and ketchup leap immediately to mind, but also try using jam, flavored cream cheese, salad dressing, marinara sauce, salsa or pesto. For convenience, you can use store-bought spreads, but if you're up for making your own, I've included a whole chapter of condiment recipes, all of which work wonderfully on panini.

As with all other areas of panini-making, experiment with condiments, using them individually and in combination, and learn what truly delights your taste buds. You might be surprised by what works, as I was when I accidentally created Turkey in a Jam Panini (page 99) which pairs turkey with raspberry jam — what an amazing treat!

Lighten up!

I make it a rule to work out at least five to six times a week, and I insist on making healthy food choices for myself and my family. Whenever I can, I use lower-fat and reduced-calorie options, such as low-fat mayonnaise and salad dressings, reduced-fat cheeses and lean meats. I also like to double up on veggies, focusing on those that possess a deep, rich color, such as spinach, carrots and beets. I adore every recipe in this book, and I know I can lighten up every single one in a way that still pleases my palate.

That being said, I also believe we all need to splurge sometimes and eat in moderation foods that tip the scale, so to speak. Use your best judgment when selecting ingredients and make wise decisions about when to splurge.

Breakfast and Brunch Panini

Crunchy Breakfast Panini

My friend and colleague Jennifer gave me this breakfast idea, which is quick, easy, full of protein and energy, and perfect for kids. I love the crunch of the granola, which is found in a host of flavors — or perhaps you have a favorite recipe.

Serves 2

Variations

Substitute slices of your favorite fruit for the banana.

Try cinnamon raisin, cranberry or harvest grain bagels instead of the plain bagels.

Preheat panini grill to high

2	plain bagels, split	2
1 tbsp	butter, melted	15 mL
¼ cup	crunchy peanut butter	50 mL
1	small banana, mashed	1
¼ cup	granola cereal	50 mL
2 tbsp	liquid honey	25 mL

1. Place bagels, cut side down, on a work surface and brush crusts with butter. Turn bagels over and spread bottom halves evenly with peanut butter and banana. Sprinkle with granola and drizzle with honey. Cover with top halves and press gently to pack.

2. Place sandwiches in grill, close the top plate and cook until golden brown, 3 to 4 minutes. Serve immediately.

French Toast Panini

Oh my … this is a culinary treat, if I may say so myself. I love this recipe, as you will too, if you love French toast. A honeyed cream cheese mixture, raspberry preserves and fragrant pecans are sandwiched between two slices of French bread, dipped in an egg batter and grilled to perfection.

Serves 2

Tips

For convenience, use frozen French toast slices and eliminate the egg batter portion of the recipe.

The cream cheese mixture alone is wonderful as a spread.

Variation

I love raspberry preserves, but you can substitute any flavor your family enjoys.

Preheat panini grill to high

¼ cup	cream cheese, softened	50 mL
2 tbsp	chopped pecans, toasted (see tip, page 37)	25 mL
1 tsp	honey	5 mL
4	slices French bread (½-inch/1 cm thick slices)	4
½ cup	raspberry preserves or jam	125 mL
1 tbsp	butter, melted	15 mL
1	egg	1
1 tbsp	milk	15 mL
Dash	vanilla extract	Dash
1 tsp	confectioner's (icing) sugar	5 mL
¼ tsp	ground cinnamon	1 mL

1. In a bowl, combine cream cheese, pecans and honey. Spread cream cheese mixture evenly over two bread slices. Spread raspberry preserves over the remaining two slices. Press the two halves together to pack.

2. In a shallow bowl, whisk together egg, milk and vanilla. Dip both sides of each sandwich in egg mixture. Discard any excess egg mixture.

3. In a small bowl, combine confectioner's sugar and cinnamon; set aside.

4. Place sandwiches in grill, close the top plate and cook until golden brown, 3 to 4 minutes. Sift sugar mixture over each panini. Serve immediately.

Denver Egg Panini

This recipe is based on the famous Denver omelet, flavorful with ham, Cheddar cheese and sautéed green peppers and onions.

Serves 2

Tips

Scrambling the eggs in the same pan you used to sauté the vegetables and ham adds more flavor to the eggs.

For more color, use red or yellow bell peppers or a combination.

Preheat panini grill to high

2 tsp	olive oil	10 mL
½ cup	chopped green bell pepper	125 mL
¼ cup	chopped onion	50 mL
½ cup	diced baked ham (2 oz/60 g)	125 mL
2 tsp	butter	10 mL
2	eggs, beaten	2
Pinch	salt	Pinch
Pinch	freshly ground black pepper	Pinch
4	slices sourdough bread (½-inch/1 cm thick slices)	4
1 tbsp	butter, melted	15 mL
½ cup	shredded Cheddar cheese	125 mL

1. In a nonstick skillet, heat oil over medium–high heat. Add green pepper and onion; sauté until tender, about 5 minutes. Add ham and sauté until heated through, 3 to 4 minutes. Transfer to a plate and keep warm.

2. In the same pan, melt the 2 tsp (10 mL) butter over medium heat. Add eggs, salt and pepper; scramble until eggs are desired consistency. Remove from heat and stir in ham mixture.

3. Brush one side of each bread slice with melted butter. Place on a work surface, buttered side down. Divide eggs evenly between two bread slices and top with cheese. Cover with top halves and press gently to pack.

4. Place sandwiches in grill, close the top plate and cook until golden brown, 3 to 4 minutes. Serve immediately.

Benedict Panini

One of my all-time favorite breakfast recipes is the classic eggs Benedict. I use the freshest ingredients, including homemade hollandaise sauce.

Serves 2

Tips

To poach eggs, add 3 inches (7.5 cm) of water to a large saucepan. Bring to a boil, then reduce heat to simmer. Add ½ tsp (2 mL) vinegar. Break eggs into a bowl, one at a time, and carefully slip into the water, as close as possible to the surface. Simmer for 3 to 5 minutes, or to desired degree of doneness. Remove with a slotted spoon.

Blanch asparagus by cooking in boiling salted water until bright green, about 30 seconds. Remove from water with a slotted spoon or mesh strainer and plunge into ice water to stop the cooking process. Drain.

Serve with seasonal fresh fruit and, for special entertaining, a refreshing mimosa made with freshly squeezed orange juice.

Variation

I love the flavor and elegance of the asparagus spears, but if you are not a fan, you can omit them or substitute sautéed fresh spinach.

Preheat panini grill to high

4	thin slices Canadian bacon	4
2	sourdough English muffins, split	2
1 tbsp	butter, melted	15 mL
2	eggs, poached (see tip, at left)	2
4	spears asparagus, blanched (see tip, at left)	4
	Classic Hollandaise (see recipe, page 241)	
Dash	paprika	Dash

1. Arrange bacon on bottom grill plate, close the top plate and cook until crispy, 1 to 2 minutes. Remove and set aside. Wipe grill plates clean.

2. Place muffins on a work surface and brush both the cut and crust sides with melted butter. Place in grill, close the top plate and cook until golden brown, 3 to 4 minutes. Remove from grill and place bottom halves on two plates. Layer each with bacon, egg and asparagus. Drizzle with hollandaise and sprinkle with paprika. Serve with top halves immediately.

Fried Egg and Italian Sausage Panini

Savory Italian sausage, sautéed and combined with eggs fried to perfection, is show-stopping with pepper Jack cheese and a sprinkle of chives, all sandwiched between fresh ciabatta rolls.

Serves 2

Tip

I love spicy food, so when making this for myself I use hot Italian sausage. When preparing this recipe for the masses, I use mild Italian sausage and opt for a less spicy cheese.

Variations

If you prefer, you can poach or scramble the eggs rather than frying them. You can also try scrambling the eggs with the sautéed sausage for incredible flavor.

Try sourdough English muffins instead of the ciabatta rolls.

Preheat panini grill to high

4 oz	Italian sausage (bulk or with casings removed)	125 g
1 tbsp	butter	15 mL
2	eggs	2
Pinch	salt	Pinch
Pinch	freshly ground black pepper	Pinch
2	ciabatta rolls, split	2
1 tbsp	butter, melted	15 mL
2 oz	pepper Jack cheese, thinly sliced	60 g
2 tbsp	chopped fresh chives	25 mL
	Salsa	

1. In a small nonstick skillet, over medium–high heat, sauté sausage, breaking up with spoon, until no longer pink, about 5 minutes. Transfer to a plate and keep warm. Drain fat.

2. In the same pan, melt the 1 tbsp (15 mL) butter over medium heat. Crack eggs into the pan and cook until whites are set but yolks are still runny. Season with salt and pepper. Flip eggs with a rubber spatula and cook until yolks are set. Remove from heat.

3. Meanwhile, place ciabatta rolls on a work surface and brush both the crust and cut sides with melted butter. Place in grill, close the top plate and cook until golden brown, 3 to 4 minutes. Remove from grill and place bottom halves on two plates. Layer with cheese, sausage and eggs. Sprinkle with chives and cover with top halves. Serve immediately with salsa.

Breakfast On the Go Panini

What is better in the morning than a fast and easy breakfast sandwich? English muffins are sturdy, hold filling well and taste wonderful, especially after toasting.

Serves 2

Tip

For faster service, scramble the eggs the night before and reheat in the microwave, being careful not to overcook them.

Variations

I also enjoy thinly sliced hard-boiled eggs in this sandwich.

Sprinkle the eggs with a bit of paprika before grilling the sandwich. I love the flavor of smoked paprika.

Preheat panini grill to high

4	slices Canadian bacon	4
2 tsp	butter	10 mL
2	eggs	2
Pinch	salt	Pinch
Pinch	freshly ground black pepper	Pinch
2	English muffins, split	2
1 tbsp	butter, melted	15 mL
2 oz	Cheddar cheese, sliced	60 g

1. Arrange bacon on bottom grill plate, close the top plate and grill until crispy, 1 to 2 minutes. Remove and set aside. Wipe grill plates clean.

2. In a nonstick skillet, melt the 2 tsp (10 mL) butter over medium heat. Crack eggs into the pan and cook until whites are set but yolks are still runny. Season with salt and pepper. Flip eggs with a rubber spatula and cook until yolks are set. Remove from heat.

3. Place muffins, cut side down, on a work surface and brush crusts with melted butter. Turn muffins over and, on the bottom half of each muffin, evenly layer with bacon, cheese and egg. Cover with top halves and press gently to pack.

4. Place sandwiches in grill, close the top plate and cook until golden brown, 3 to 4 minutes. Serve immediately.

Apple, Cheddar and Bacon Bagels

The fragrant goodness of apples and Cheddar cheese, adorned with crisp bacon and grilled to toasty perfection in a cinnamon raisin bagel, will be the perfect start to your day.

Serves 2

Tip
Other apple varieties that would work well include Granny Smith, Golden Delicious and Jonathan.

Variation
Substitute your favorite bagels for the cinnamon raisin.

Preheat panini grill to high

1 tbsp	butter	15 mL
1	McIntosh apple, peeled and sliced	1
1 tsp	light brown sugar	5 mL
2	cinnamon raisin bagels, split	2
2 tbsp	butter, melted	25 mL
2 tbsp	cream cheese, softened	25 mL
2 oz	Cheddar cheese, sliced	60 g
2	slices bacon, cooked crisp and crumbled	2

1. In a nonstick skillet, melt the 1 tbsp (15 mL) butter over medium–high heat. Add apple and brown sugar; sauté until tender, 3 to 4 minutes. Remove from heat and keep warm.

2. Place bagels, cut side down, on a work surface and brush crusts with melted butter. Turn bagels over and spread cream cheese evenly on the bottom halves. Top evenly with cooked apples, Cheddar cheese and bacon. Cover with top halves and press gently to pack.

3. Place sandwiches in grill, close the top plate and cook until golden brown, 3 to 4 minutes. Serve immediately.

Bacon, Tomato and Swiss Panini

Fresh tomatoes, layered with bacon, Swiss cheese and perfectly scrambled eggs, are the right start for a great day!

Serves 2

Tips

This is the perfect panini to take on the go, so wrap it up and head out the door!

I have used liquid egg substitute in this recipe, and I love the ease of this convenience item.

Preheat panini grill to high

2 tsp	butter	10 mL
2	eggs, beaten	2
Pinch	salt	Pinch
Pinch	freshly ground black pepper	Pinch
4	slices whole wheat bread (½-inch/1 cm thick slices)	4
1 tbsp	butter, melted	15 mL
2 oz	Swiss cheese, thinly sliced	60 g
4	slices bacon, cooked crisp	4
4	thin slices tomato	4

1. In a nonstick skillet, melt the 2 tsp (10 mL) butter over medium heat. Add eggs, salt and pepper; scramble until eggs are desired consistency. Remove from heat.

2. Brush one side of each bread slice with melted butter. Place on a work surface, buttered side down. Divide eggs evenly between two bread slices and top with cheese, bacon and tomato. Cover with top halves and press gently to pack.

3. Place sandwiches in grill, close the top plate and cook until golden brown, 3 to 4 minutes. Serve immediately.

Grilled Mushroom Breakfast Quesadillas

Sautéed mushrooms are enhanced with the flavor of roasted red peppers, freshly scrambled eggs and melted Monterey Jack cheese.

Serves 2

Tip

I used button mushrooms, but cremini, shiitake or your favorite variety will also work well. For convenience, purchase sliced mushrooms or a stir-fry mushroom mix.

Variation

If you can find flavored flour tortillas, give them a try. I found that herbed tortillas worked very well, as did rosemary-flavored tortillas.

Preheat panini grill to high

2 tsp	olive oil	10 mL
6 oz	mushrooms, sliced	175 g
	Vegetable cooking spray	
2	eggs	2
Pinch	salt	Pinch
Pinch	freshly ground black pepper	Pinch
2	8-inch (20 cm) flour tortillas	2
¼ cup	sliced roasted red bell peppers	50 mL
½ cup	shredded Monterey Jack cheese	125 mL

1. In a nonstick skillet, heat oil over medium–high heat. Add mushrooms and sauté until tender, about 5 minutes. Transfer to a plate and keep warm.

2. Coat pan with cooking spray and reduce heat to medium. Add eggs, salt and pepper; scramble until eggs are desired consistency. Remove from heat.

3. Coat one side of each tortilla with cooking spray. Place one tortilla, coated side down, on a work surface. Layer with mushrooms, eggs, roasted peppers and cheese. Cover with remaining tortilla, coated side up, and press gently to pack.

4. Place quesadilla in grill, close the top plate and cook until golden brown, 3 to 4 minutes. Cut in half and serve immediately.

Smoked Salmon Quesadillas

So much fresh flavor is added when dill is sprinkled over smoked salmon, red onion, cream cheese and shredded provolone. Surround this breakfast creation in a tortilla and grill for an upscale breakfast quesadilla.

Serves 1 or 2

Tip

I recommend using fresh dill, but ½ tsp (2 mL) dried will work if you don't have fresh.

Variation

Try chive-flavored cream cheese, often sold in grocery stores.

Preheat panini grill to high

2	8-inch (20 cm) flour tortillas	2
	Vegetable cooking spray	
1 tbsp	cream cheese, softened	15 mL
2 oz	smoked salmon, thinly sliced	60 g
½ cup	shredded provolone cheese	125 mL
1 tbsp	finely chopped red onion	15 mL
1 tsp	chopped fresh dill	5 mL

1. Coat one side of each tortilla with cooking spray. Place one tortilla, coated side down, on a work surface. Spread with cream cheese and layer with salmon, provolone cheese, onion and dill. Cover with remaining tortilla, coated side up, and press gently to pack.

2. Place quesadilla in grill, close the top plate and cook until golden brown, 3 to 4 minutes. Cut in half and serve immediately.

Smoked Salmon, Red Onion, Cream Cheese and Caper Panini

This ingredient lineup is full of fresh flavors that complement salmon so well: crisp red onion and cream cheese, accented with chives and capers. I call it the bagel panini. Split bagels are wonderful in almost any of my panini recipes. Just make sure the ingredients are proportioned to the bagel; you may have to do a bit of trimming, but it's worth the effort.

Serves 2

Variations

Try dill-, onion- or garlic-flavored cream cheese.

A chopped hard-boiled egg would make a great addition.

Bagels come in many different varieties, so experiment to find your favorite flavor combination.

Preheat panini grill to high

2	plain bagels, split	2
1 tbsp	olive oil	15 mL
¼ cup	cream cheese, softened	50 mL
6 oz	smoked salmon, thinly sliced	175 g
2 tbsp	finely chopped red onion	25 mL
1 tbsp	chopped fresh chives	15 mL
1 tsp	drained capers	5 mL

1. Place bagels, cut side down, on a work surface and brush crusts with oil. Turn bagels over and spread evenly with cream cheese. On bottom halves, evenly layer with salmon, onion, chives and capers. Cover with top halves and press gently to pack.

2. Place sandwiches in grill, close the top plate and cook until golden brown, 3 to 4 minutes. Serve immediately.

Corned Beef Bagels

Corned beef marries well with pizza sauce and fontina cheese, grilled in a plain bagel or a bagel of your choice.

Serves 2

Tip

Corned beef is usually brisket cured or pickled in a seasoned brine, and can be found at most supermarket delis. In Ireland, it is traditionally served on Easter Sunday and on St. Patrick's Day.

Variation

Mozzarella cheese makes a nice substitute for or addition to the fontina.

Preheat panini grill to high

2	plain bagels, split	2
1 tbsp	butter, melted	15 mL
½ cup	pizza sauce or marinara sauce	125 mL
2 oz	corned beef, thinly sliced	60 g
½ cup	shredded fontina cheese	125 mL

1. Place bagels, cut side down, on a work surface and brush crusts with butter. Turn bagels over and spread evenly with pizza sauce. On bottom halves, evenly layer with beef and fontina. Cover with top halves and press gently to pack.

2. Place sandwiches in grill, close the top plate and cook until golden brown, 3 to 4 minutes. Serve immediately.

Veggie Brunch Panini

This crisp, fresh panini, with vegetables, hummus and cream cheese, is great any time of day, but especially for breakfast or brunch.

Serves 2

Tip

Hummus is a popular sandwich spread, dip and pizza topping. There are now so many hummus varieties on the market, you are sure to find one you love.

Variations

Substitute your favorite vegetables in this recipe and make it your own!

Look for cream cheese flavored with garlic, roasted pepper or herbs.

Preheat panini grill to high

2	plain bagels, split	2
1 tbsp	butter, melted	15 mL
2 tbsp	hummus	25 mL
2 tbsp	cream cheese, softened	25 mL
4	thin slices red onion	4
½	small green bell pepper, thinly sliced	½
½ cup	thinly sliced cucumber	125 mL
½ cup	alfalfa sprouts	125 mL
Pinch	salt	Pinch
Pinch	freshly ground black pepper	Pinch

1. Place bagels, cut side down, on a work surface and brush crusts with butter. Turn bagels over and spread bottom halves evenly with hummus. Spread top halves with cream cheese. On bottom halves, evenly layer with onion, green pepper, cucumber and alfalfa sprouts. Sprinkle with salt and pepper. Cover with top halves and press gently to pack.

2. Place sandwiches in grill, close the top plate and cook until golden brown, 3 to 4 minutes. Serve immediately.

Vegetarian Panini

continued, next page...

Mozzarella Panini

This panini is utterly satisfying, with the perfect combination of flavors.

Serves 2

Tips

Serve with tomato soup for the perfect meal.

Variation

For a lower-fat version of this sandwich, use low-fat mayonnaise and part-skim cheese, and use cooking spray in place of the butter.

Preheat panini grill to high

4	slices sourdough bread (½-inch/1 cm thick slices)	4
1 tbsp	butter, melted	15 mL
2 tbsp	Sun-Dried Tomato Mayonnaise (see recipe, page 236)	25 mL
4 oz	mozzarella cheese, thinly sliced	125 g
¼ cup	baby spinach leaves	50 mL

1. Brush one side of each bread slice with butter. Place on a work surface, buttered side down, and spread with mayonnaise. On bottom halves, evenly layer with mozzarella and spinach. Cover with top halves and press gently to pack.

2. Place sandwiches in grill, close the top plate and cook until golden brown, 3 to 4 minutes. Serve immediately.

Four-Cheese Panini

If I were stranded on a deserted island, I could survive on cheese alone. For this recipe, I have chosen four of my favorites, all of which have wonderful melting properties.

Serves 2

Tips

If you have only one or two of these cheeses, go ahead and make the sandwich anyway. With all four, this is a big cheese sandwich!

Fontina and Gouda have similar melting properties and can be used interchangeably.

Any bread will work in this recipe — try your favorite.

Preheat panini grill to high

4	slices sourdough bread (1-inch/2.5 cm thick slices)	4
1 tbsp	olive oil	15 mL
2 oz	mozzarella cheese, thinly sliced	60 g
2 oz	smoked Cheddar cheese, thinly sliced	60 g
2 oz	fontina cheese, thinly sliced	60 g
2 oz	provolone cheese, thinly sliced	60 g

1. Brush one side of each bread slice with oil. Place two slices on a work surface, oiled side down, and evenly layer with mozzarella, Cheddar, fontina and provolone. Cover with top halves, oiled side up, and press gently to pack.

2. Place sandwiches in grill, close the top plate and cook until golden brown, 3 to 4 minutes. Serve immediately.

Brie and Fontina Panini with Jalapeño Jelly

This panini has two of my favorite cheeses: Brie and fontina. The sweet-tart jalapeño jelly adds a bit of a kick.

Serves 2

Tips

For an easy appetizer, remove the rind from a wheel of Brie. Spread jalapeño jelly on top and serve with water crackers.

Warming the jalapeño jelly makes it much easier to spread.

Preheat panini grill to high

2	ciabatta rolls	2
1 tbsp	butter, melted	15 mL
¼ cup	jalapeño jelly	50 mL
2 oz	Brie cheese, rind removed, thinly sliced	60 g
2 oz	fontina cheese, thinly sliced	60 g

1. Brush both the cut and crust sides of rolls with butter. Place on a work surface, crust side down.

2. In a microwave, warm jalapeño jelly on High for 30 seconds. Spread evenly over cut sides of rolls. On bottom halves, evenly layer with Brie and fontina. Cover with top halves and press gently to pack.

3. Place sandwiches in grill, close the top plate and cook until golden brown, 3 to 4 minutes. Serve immediately.

Basil and Provolone Panini

Provolone is a perfect cooking cheese that works remarkably well in panini.

Serves 2

Tips

As provolone ages, it becomes harder in texture, perfect for grating.

Bolillo rolls — one of the most popular breads in Mexico — are made with a basic dough similar to French baguette dough. The rolls have a crispy crust with a soft, chewy crumb. If you can't find them, you can substitute submarine rolls, sourdough rolls or hoagie rolls.

Preheat panini grill to high

2	bolillo rolls, split	2
1 tbsp	olive oil	15 mL
2 tsp	mayonnaise	10 mL
2 oz	provolone cheese, thinly sliced	60 g
¼ cup	thinly sliced fresh basil	50 mL
¼ cup	thinly sliced red bell pepper	50 mL

1. Place rolls, cut side down, on a work surface and brush crusts with oil. Turn rolls over and spread evenly with mayonnaise. On bottom halves, evenly layer with provolone, basil and red pepper. Cover with top halves and press gently to pack.

2. Place sandwiches in grill, close the top plate and cook until golden brown, 3 to 4 minutes. Serve immediately.

French Toast Panini (page 15)

Benedict Panini (page 17)

Mango, Poblano and Cream Cheese Panini (page 36)

Spinach, Pear and Walnut Panini with Feta (page 37)

Spinach, Goat Cheese and Sun-Dried Tomato Panini (page 41)

Greek Veggie Panini (page 53)

Tuna and Artichoke Panini (page 63)

Shrimp Club Panini (page 80)

Uptown Grilled Cheese Panini

This is the ultimate grilled cheese sandwich, filled with melted smoked Cheddar cheese, creamy Brie, fresh tomato and a duo of bell peppers.

Serves 2

Variations

For a more peppery bite, substitute arugula for the spinach.

If you have different cheeses on hand, feel free to substitute mozzarella, fontina, Gouda or American.

Preheat panini grill to high

4	slices sourdough bread (1-inch/2.5 cm thick slices)	4
1 tbsp	olive oil	15 mL
1 tbsp	Dijon mustard	15 mL
2 oz	smoked Cheddar cheese, thinly sliced	60 g
2 oz	Brie cheese, rind removed, thinly sliced	60 g
4	thin slices tomato	4
½ cup	baby spinach leaves	125 mL
¼ cup	thinly sliced red bell pepper	50 mL
¼ cup	thinly sliced green bell pepper	50 mL
Pinch	salt	Pinch
Pinch	freshly ground black pepper	Pinch

1. Brush one side of each bread slice with oil. Place on a work surface, oiled side down, and spread with mustard. On bottom halves, evenly layer with Cheddar, Brie, tomato, spinach and red and green peppers. Sprinkle with salt and pepper. Cover with top halves and press gently to pack.

2. Place sandwiches in grill, close the top plate and cook until golden brown, 3 to 4 minutes. Serve immediately.

OMG Pimento Cheese Panini

When I was growing up, my grandmother made homemade pimento cheese — what a treat! I love the flavor combination of Cheddar, Monterey Jack and pimentos, and I hope you do too. Pimento cheese is yummy just spread on bread, but put it in a panini grill, and oh my goodness!

Serves 2

Tips

For a more pungent flavor, try sharp (old) Cheddar cheese.

If you don't like the look of the black specks of pepper, use freshly ground white pepper instead.

The pimento cheese can be made ahead and stored in an airtight container in the refrigerator for up to 1 week (if it doesn't get eaten long before!).

Variation

Lighten up this recipe by using reduced-fat cheeses and low-fat mayonnaise.

Preheat panini grill to high

1	jar (4 oz/125 mL) chopped pimentos, drained	1
1 cup	shredded mild Cheddar cheese	250 mL
1 cup	shredded Monterey Jack cheese	250 mL
1/3 cup	mayonnaise	75 mL
1/2 tsp	freshly ground black pepper	2 mL
1/4 tsp	salt	1 mL
1/4 tsp	garlic powder	1 mL
1/4 tsp	paprika	1 mL
4	slices sourdough bread (1/2-inch/1 cm thick slices)	4
1 tbsp	butter, melted	15 mL

1. In a bowl, combine pimentos, Cheddar, Monterey Jack, mayonnaise, pepper, salt, garlic powder and paprika.

2. Brush one side of each bread slice with butter. Place two slices on a work surface, buttered side down, and spread evenly with pimento cheese. Cover with top halves, buttered side up, and press gently to pack.

3. Place sandwiches in grill, close the top plate and cook until golden brown, 3 to 4 minutes. Serve immediately.

Hummus, Red Onion and Swiss Panini

Mild, delicate, sweet Swiss cheese is a perfect counterpoint to hummus and red onion.

Serves 2

Tip

Swiss cheese is often found in recipes for fondue, desserts or quiches because it has wonderful melting properties.

Preheat panini grill to high

2	8-inch (20 cm) pitas	2
1 tbsp	olive oil	15 mL
¼ cup	hummus	50 mL
2 oz	Swiss cheese, thinly sliced	60 g
4	slices red onion	4
½ cup	alfalfa sprouts	125 mL
Pinch	salt	Pinch
Pinch	freshly ground black pepper	Pinch

1. Brush one side of each pita with oil. Place one pita on a work surface, oiled side down, and spread with hummus. Layer with cheese, onion and sprouts. Sprinkle with salt and pepper. Cover with remaining pita, oiled side up, and press gently to pack.

2. Place sandwich in grill, close the top plate and cook until golden brown, 3 to 4 minutes. Cut into wedges and serve immediately.

Mango, Poblano and Cream Cheese Panini

The freshness of mango, paired with poblano peppers and cream cheese, is exceptional in this melted wonder. Enjoy this sandwich on a hot summer day with a frozen margarita!

Serves 2

Tip

If you do not care for cilantro, substitute Italian (flat-leaf) parsley or omit it.

Variation

Cubed papaya also tastes fantastic in this recipe.

Preheat panini grill to high

1	small mango, cubed	1
1	small poblano chile pepper, seeded and chopped	1
1 tbsp	chopped fresh cilantro	15 mL
2 tsp	minced red onion	10 mL
1 tbsp	freshly squeezed lime juice	15 mL
2	8- or 10-inch (20 or 25 cm) flour tortillas	2
1 tsp	butter, melted	5 mL
¼ cup	cream cheese, softened	50 mL

1. In a bowl, combine mango, poblano, cilantro, onion and lime juice.

2. Brush one side of each tortilla with butter. Place on a work surface, buttered side down, and spread cream cheese over half of each tortilla, dividing evenly and leaving a ½-inch (1 cm) border around the edges. Evenly layer mango mixture on top of cream cheese. Fold tortillas over filling, pressing gently to pack.

3. Place sandwiches in grill, close the top plate and cook until golden brown, 3 to 4 minutes. Serve immediately.

Spinach, Pear and Walnut Panini with Feta

This elegant panini features sweet Bosc pears and savory feta cheese and sage, laced with a drizzle of tart balsamic vinegar.

Serves 2

Tips

When I can't find walnut bread, I use cranberry bread, pistachio bread or challah. If you cannot find any of these, use wheat or white bread.

For the best flavor, always use fresh sage rather than dried. Cooking sage helps it develop its full flavor potential.

Roasting nuts gives them a richer, fuller flavor. To roast, spread nuts evenly on a baking sheet and roast in a 350°F (180°C) oven until fragrant and light brown, 5 to 10 minutes. Smaller nuts and seeds, such as pine nuts, chopped hazelnuts, sunflower seeds and pumpkin seeds, can be toasted in a skillet over medium-high heat. Stir constantly with a spatula or wooden spoon to keep them from burning.

Preheat panini grill to high

4	slices artisan walnut bread (½-inch/1 cm thick slices)	4
1 tbsp	butter, melted	15 mL
2 tbsp	cream cheese, softened	25 mL
1	ripe but firm Bosc pear, thinly sliced	1
2 oz	feta cheese, crumbled	60 g
½ cup	baby spinach leaves	125 mL
1 tbsp	chopped fresh sage	15 mL
1 tbsp	chopped walnuts, toasted (see tip, at left)	15 mL
1 tbsp	balsamic vinegar	15 mL

1. Brush one side of each bread slice with butter. Place two slices on a work surface, buttered side down, and spread with cream cheese. Evenly layer with pear slices, feta, spinach, sage and walnuts. Drizzle with vinegar. Cover with top halves, buttered side up, and press gently to pack.

2. Place sandwiches in grill, close the top plate and cook until golden brown, 3 to 4 minutes. Serve immediately.

Spinach, Mozzarella and Basil Pesto Panini

For a culinary treat, try using fresh buffalo mozzarella cheese, made from buffalo milk.

Serves 2

Tip
When purchasing spinach, choose leaves that are dark green and crisp. Avoid limp or damaged–looking greens and leaves with yellow spots.

Preheat panini grill to high

2 tbsp	mayonnaise	25 mL
2 tsp	basil pesto (store-bought or see recipe, page 245)	10 mL
4	slices sourdough bread (½-inch/1 cm thick slices)	4
1 tbsp	olive oil	15 mL
4 oz	mozzarella cheese, thinly sliced	125 g
½ cup	baby spinach leaves	125 mL

1. In a bowl, combine mayonnaise and pesto.

2. Brush one side of each bread slice with oil. Place on a work surface, oiled side down, and spread with mayonnaise mixture. On bottom halves, evenly layer with mozzarella and spinach. Cover with top halves and press gently to pack.

3. Place sandwiches in grill, close the top plate and cook until golden brown, 3 to 4 minutes. Serve immediately.

Spinach and Artichoke Panini

Often combined to make a delicious dip, spinach and artichoke now find a home in a panini, with support from red onion and shaved Parmesan cheese. Dense ciabatta rolls make the perfect foundation.

Serves 2

Tip

Freshly shaved Parmesan will have the best flavor, but for convenience you can use pregrated Parmesan cheese.

Preheat panini grill to high

2	ciabatta rolls, split	2
1 tbsp	olive oil	15 mL
¼ cup	cream cheese, softened	50 mL
½ cup	roughly chopped drained artichoke hearts	125 mL
½ cup	baby spinach leaves	125 mL
¼ cup	thinly sliced red onion	50 mL
2 tbsp	shaved Parmesan cheese	25 mL

1. Place rolls, cut side down, on a work surface and brush crusts with oil. Turn rolls over and spread cream cheese over the bottom halves. Evenly layer with artichokes, spinach, red onion and Parmesan. Cover with top halves and press gently to pack.

2. Place sandwiches in grill, close the top plate and cook until golden brown, 3 to 4 minutes. Serve immediately.

Spinach Lasagna Panini

In this panini, all the wonderful flavors of spinach lasagna are melted together inside ciabatta rolls, so you can eat your lasagna with your hands!

Serves 2

Tip

When substituting fresh herbs for dried or vice versa, keep in mind this rule of thumb: 1 tsp (5 mL) dried herbs equals 1 tbsp (15 mL) chopped fresh.

Preheat panini grill to high

¼ cup	ricotta cheese	50 mL
1 tbsp	freshly grated Parmesan cheese	15 mL
Pinch	dried oregano	Pinch
Pinch	dried basil	Pinch
2	ciabatta rolls, split	2
1 tbsp	olive oil	15 mL
¼ cup	pizza sauce or marinara sauce	50 mL
½ cup	baby spinach leaves	125 mL
½ cup	shredded mozzarella cheese	125 mL
Pinch	salt	Pinch
Pinch	freshly ground black pepper	Pinch

1. In a bowl, combine ricotta, Parmesan, oregano and basil.

2. Place rolls, cut side down, on a work surface and brush crusts with oil. Turn rolls over and spread pizza sauce over the bottom halves. Evenly layer with ricotta mixture, spinach and mozzarella. Sprinkle with salt and pepper. Cover with top halves and press gently to pack.

3. Place sandwiches in grill, close the top plate and cook until golden brown, 3 to 4 minutes. Serve immediately.

Spinach, Goat Cheese and Sun-Dried Tomato Panini

The combination of goat cheese and ricotta with a blending of Italian seasonings is perfect for this panini.

Serves 2

Tips

Store spinach in a plastic bag and refrigerate for no more than 3 days. Spinach has a tendency to be gritty, so make sure to rinse it thoroughly before using.

Thoroughly drain the sun-dried tomatoes to ensure that the bread doesn't get soggy.

Preheat panini grill to high

¼ cup	goat cheese, softened	50 mL
¼ cup	ricotta cheese	50 mL
¼ tsp	Italian seasoning	1 mL
4	slices sourdough bread (½-inch/1 cm thick slices)	4
1 tbsp	olive oil	15 mL
1 cup	baby spinach leaves	250 mL
¼ cup	sliced drained oil-packed sun-dried tomatoes	50 mL
¼ cup	shaved Parmesan cheese	50 mL
Pinch	freshly ground black pepper	Pinch

1. In a bowl, combine goat cheese, ricotta and Italian seasoning.

2. Brush one side of each bread slice with oil. Place two slices on a work surface, oiled side down, and evenly layer with goat cheese mixture, spinach, tomatoes and Parmesan. Sprinkle with pepper. Cover with top halves, oiled side up, and press gently to pack.

3. Place sandwiches in grill, close the top plate and cook until golden brown, 3 to 4 minutes. Serve immediately.

Popeye Panini

This recipe reminds me of the cartoon characters I grew up with: Popeye and Olive Oyl. I could have put sweet peas in this — on second thought, maybe not.

Serves 2

Tip

Rubbing garlic on bread, then heating the bread, creates great garlic flavor.

Preheat panini grill to high

2	ciabatta rolls, split	2
2 tbsp	olive oil, divided	25 mL
1	clove garlic, halved	1
3 oz	mozzarella cheese, thinly sliced	90 g
6	thin slices tomato	6
½ cup	baby spinach leaves	125 mL
Pinch	salt	Pinch
Pinch	freshly ground black pepper	Pinch

1. Brush both the cut and crust sides of rolls with 1 tbsp (15 mL) of the oil. Place on a work surface, crust side down. Rub cut sides with garlic, then discard cloves. On bottom halves, evenly layer with mozzarella, tomato and spinach. Sprinkle with salt and pepper and drizzle with the remaining oil. Cover with top halves and press gently to pack.

2. Place sandwiches in grill, close the top plate and cook until golden brown, 3 to 4 minutes. Serve immediately.

Tomato, Basil and Mozzarella Panini

Using fresh ingredients is key in any recipe, but especially in this one. I used an herb-flavored focaccia that had been freshly baked at my local supermarket.

Serves 2

Tip

Focaccia is an Italian flatbread flavored with various ingredients, such as herbs, olive oil, tomatoes, cheeses, olives, roasted pepper and eggplant.

Preheat panini grill to high

2	4-inch (10 cm) focaccia, halved horizontally	2
1 tbsp	olive oil	15 mL
2 tbsp	Basil Mayonnaise (see recipe, page 236)	25 mL
4	thin slices tomato	4
½ cup	shredded mozzarella cheese	125 mL

1. Place focaccia, cut side down, on a work surface and brush crusts with oil. Turn focaccia over and spread with mayonnaise. On bottom halves, evenly layer with tomato and mozzarella. Cover with top halves and press gently to pack.

2. Place sandwiches in grill, close the top plate and cook until golden brown, 3 to 4 minutes. Serve immediately.

Tomato, Feta and Basil Panini

Use basil fresh from your garden if at all possible for the wonderful spread inside this panini.

Serves 2

Tips

I often double the cheese mixture and serve it as a dip with gourmet crackers. It can be stored in an airtight container in the refrigerator for up to 5 days.

I have used heirloom tomatoes of various colors in this recipe, with incredible results.

Preheat panini grill to high

2 oz	feta cheese, crumbled	60 g
2 tbsp	chopped fresh basil	25 mL
2 tbsp	mayonnaise	25 mL
Pinch	salt	Pinch
Pinch	freshly ground black pepper	Pinch
4	slices sourdough bread (½-inch/1 cm thick slices)	4
1 tbsp	olive oil	15 mL
4	thin slices tomato	4

1. In a bowl, combine feta, basil, mayonnaise, salt and pepper.

2. Brush one side of each bread slice with oil. Place two slices on a work surface, oiled side down, and evenly layer with cheese mixture and tomato. Cover with top halves, oiled side up, and press gently to pack.

3. Place sandwiches in grill, close the top plate and cook until golden brown, 3 to 4 minutes. Serve immediately.

The Melted Tomato Panini

Many years ago, when writing a cookbook was just a dream, I visited a wonderful little bistro called The Melted Tomato. I dined al fresco, munching on melted tomato crostini. Now I present to you the melted tomato in the form of a panini.

Serves 2

Tips

Focaccia is an Italian flatbread traditionally flavored with olive oil and salt and often topped with herbs, onions or other flavorings. It is wonderful in panini recipes. You can also use two 4–inch (10 cm) focaccia instead of 1 large.

Use globe tomatoes when they're in season; in the off-season, opt for plum (Roma) tomatoes.

Preheat panini grill to high

1	10-inch (25 cm) focaccia, halved horizontally	1
1 tbsp	butter, melted	15 mL
2 tbsp	aïoli (store-bought or see recipe, page 240)	25 mL
6	thin slices tomato	6
2 oz	Brie cheese, rind removed, thinly sliced	60 g
Pinch	freshly ground black pepper	Pinch

1. Place focaccia, cut side down, on a work surface and brush crusts with butter. Turn focaccia over and spread with aïoli. On bottom half, evenly layer with tomato and Brie. Sprinkle with pepper. Cover with top half and press gently to pack.

2. Place sandwich in grill, close the top plate and cook until golden brown, 3 to 4 minutes. Cut in half and serve immediately.

Two-Cheese Tomato Panini

Two of my favorite cheeses, along with honey Dijon, make this tomato sandwich a delicious treat.

Serves 2

Variation
When you have a craving for a simple cheese sandwich, just omit the tomato.

Preheat panini grill to high

4	slices country white bread (½-inch/1 cm thick slices)	4
1 tbsp	butter, melted	15 mL
1 tbsp	honey Dijon mustard	15 mL
1 oz	fontina cheese, thinly sliced	30 g
1 oz	Cheddar cheese, thinly sliced	30 g
4	thin slices tomato	4

1. Brush one side of each bread slice with butter. Place on a work surface, buttered sides down, and spread with mustard. On bottom halves, evenly layer with fontina, Cheddar and tomato. Cover with top halves and press gently to pack.

2. Place sandwiches in grill, close the top plate and cook until golden brown, 3 to 4 minutes. Serve immediately.

Red Onion, Tomato and Fontina Panini

Spicy mustard and aïoli are the perfect complements to fresh red onion, tomato and fontina cheese.

Serves 2

Tips

Fontina, originally produced in Italy, is a ripened cheese of variable texture and flavor.

In mesclun mix, also called field greens or spring salad mix, you might find arugula, dandelion, frisée, mizuna, mâche, radicchio, oak leaf, endive and sorrel. When wrapped in plastic and stored in the vegetable crisper, the greens will stay fresh for a week.

Preheat panini grill to high

2	ciabatta rolls, split	2
1 tbsp	olive oil	15 mL
1 tbsp	aïoli (store-bought or see recipe, page 240)	15 mL
1 tbsp	spicy mustard	15 mL
2 oz	fontina cheese, thinly sliced	60 g
4	thin slices tomato	4
4	thin slices red onion	4
2	pepperoncini peppers, thinly sliced	2
½ cup	mesclun mix	125 mL

1. Place rolls, cut side down, on a work surface and brush crusts with oil. Turn rolls over and spread aïoli over the bottom halves. Spread mustard over the top halves. On bottom halves, evenly layer with fontina, tomato, onion, peppers and mesclun mix. Cover with top halves and press gently to pack

2. Place sandwiches in grill, close the top plate and cook until golden brown, 3 to 4 minutes. Serve immediately.

Grilled Eggplant, Tomato and Swiss Panini

Grilled eggplant and onion, which sweeten and soften as they grill, make a true sensation once sandwiched between slices of Italian bread and topped with tomato slices and Swiss cheese.

Serves 2

Tip

Choose an eggplant that has shiny, smooth skin, without blemishes, and a green stem without brown spots. The skin should be resilient and bounce back when you apply pressure, and the eggplant should feel heavy for its size.

Preheat panini grill to high

1	small eggplant (4 to 6 oz/125 to 175 g), thinly sliced	1
1	small onion, cut into thin slices	1
1 tbsp	olive oil	15 mL
Pinch	salt	Pinch
Pinch	freshly ground black pepper	Pinch
4	slices Italian bread (½-inch/1 cm thick slices)	4
1 tbsp	butter, melted	15 mL
2 tbsp	Basil Mayonnaise (see recipe, page 236)	25 mL
1	plum (Roma) tomato, thinly sliced	1
2 oz	Swiss cheese, thinly sliced	60 g

1. Brush both sides of the eggplant and onion with oil and sprinkle with salt and pepper. Arrange on bottom grill plate, close the top plate and grill until eggplant is tender and grill-marked, 3 to 5 minutes. Remove, separate onion rings and keep warm. Wipe grill plates clean.

2. Brush one side of each bread slice with butter. Place on a work surface, buttered side down, and spread with mayonnaise. On bottom halves, evenly layer with grilled eggplant and onion, tomato and cheese. Cover with top halves and press gently to pack.

3. Place sandwiches on grill, close the top plate and cook until golden brown, 3 to 4 minutes. Serve immediately.

Sun-Dried Tomato, Basil Pesto and Shaved Parmesan Panini

This panini, full of the flavors of Italy, is also fabulous with rosemary focaccia as a base.

Serves 2

Tips

When I walk into a bakery and find freshly baked sourdough bread, I always plan for a panini. The flavor of sourdough is amazing in just about any sandwich.

To save time, purchase julienned sun-dried tomatoes.

Preheat panini grill to high

4	slices sourdough bread (½-inch/1 cm thick slices)	4
1 tbsp	olive oil	15 mL
¼ cup	basil pesto (store-bought or see recipe, page 245)	50 mL
2 oz	mozzarella cheese, thinly sliced	60 g
¼ cup	shaved Parmesan cheese	50 mL
⅓ cup	thinly sliced drained oil-packed sun-dried tomatoes	75 mL

1. Brush one side of each bread slice with oil. Place on a work surface, oiled side down, and spread with pesto. On bottom halves, evenly layer with mozzarella, Parmesan and tomatoes. Cover with top halves and press gently to pack.

2. Place sandwiches in grill, close the top plate and cook until golden brown, 3 to 4 minutes. Serve immediately.

Goat Cheese and Sun-Dried Tomato Panini

Creamy goat cheese binds sun-dried tomatoes and fresh basil to create a delicate sandwich that melts beautifully and tastes even better.

Serves 2

Tip

Goat cheese, also called chèvre, is a pure white cheese made from goat's milk. It is available in round, drum and log shapes.

Preheat panini grill to high

4	slices sourdough bread (½-inch/1 cm thick slices)	4
1 tbsp	olive oil	15 mL
3 oz	goat cheese, softened	90 g
¼ cup	sliced drained oil-packed sun-dried tomatoes	50 mL
4	large basil leaves	4
Pinch	dried Italian seasoning	Pinch

1. Brush one side of each bread slice with oil. Place on a work surface, oiled side down, and spread with goat cheese. On bottom halves, evenly layer with tomatoes and basil. Sprinkle with Italian seasoning. Cover with top halves and press gently to pack.

2. Place sandwiches in grill, close the top plate and cook until golden brown, 3 to 4 minutes. Serve immediately.

Hummus, Veggie and Arugula Panini

Hummus is a wonderful addition to almost any panini recipe, especially when paired with cucumber, arugula and bell pepper. What an amazing flavor combination!

Serves 2

Tips

Arugula is a bitter salad green with a peppery, mustardy flavor. It is very similar in appearance to radish leaves and can be found in specialty produce markets and some supermarkets.

I used a red bell pepper for this recipe, but any color will work. Red bell peppers, which are the most mature, provide the sweetest flavor.

Hummus is a smooth, thick mixture of mashed chickpeas, tahini, oil, lemon juice, and garlic. It is most commonly used as a dip for pitas.

Preheat panini grill to high

6	thin slices cucumber	6
½ cup	arugula	125 mL
¼ cup	thinly sliced bell pepper	50 mL
1 tbsp	freshly grated Parmesan cheese	15 mL
2 tbsp	Basic Vinaigrette (see recipe, page 234)	25 mL
2	Italian rolls, split	2
1 tbsp	olive oil	15 mL
¼ cup	hummus	50 mL
1	small avocado, thinly sliced	1
2 tbsp	sliced drained oil-packed sun-dried tomatoes	25 mL
Pinch	salt	Pinch
Pinch	freshly ground black pepper	Pinch

1. In a bowl, toss cucumber, arugula, bell pepper and Parmesan with vinaigrette.

2. Place rolls, cut side down, on a work surface and brush crusts with oil. Turn rolls over and spread hummus over the bottom halves. Evenly layer with cucumber mixture, avocado and tomatoes. Sprinkle with salt and pepper. Cover with top halves and press gently to pack.

3. Place sandwiches in grill, close the top plate and cook until golden brown, 3 to 4 minutes. Serve immediately.

Super Veggie Panini

Some days, you just want the crunch of veggies, and you will find it in this recipe. During the warm summer months, enjoy the freshness of the season, packaged into a panini.

Serves 2

Tips

I often purchase flavored olive oils. Garlic-flavored olive oil, one of my favorites, gives amazing flavor to grilled bread.

For convenience, you can use any bottled vinaigrette, but it's so easy to make your own!

Mesclun is a mixture of leafy greens, often including young lettuces.

Preheat panini grill to high

1	6-inch (15 cm) French baguette, split and cut in half	1
1 tbsp	olive oil	15 mL
2 tbsp	mayonnaise	25 mL
2 oz	Swiss cheese, thinly sliced	60 g
8	thin slices cucumber	8
6	thin slices tomato	6
1	small avocado, thinly sliced	1
½ cup	mesclun mix	125 mL
2 tbsp	Basic Vinaigrette (see recipe, page 234)	25 mL

1. Place baguette halves, cut side down, on a work surface and brush crusts with oil. Turn baguettes over and spread with mayonnaise. On bottom halves, evenly layer with cheese, cucumber, tomato, avocado and mesclun mix. Drizzle with vinaigrette. Cover with top halves and press gently to pack.

2. Place sandwiches in grill, close the top plate and cook until golden brown, 3 to 4 minutes. Serve immediately.

Greek Veggie Panini

The freshness of cucumber, tomato and red onion combines with the salty flavor of kalamata olives in this traditional Greek recipe.

Serves 2

Tip

Kalamata olives are packed in vinegar and cured, producing a rich, sour flavor. They're great served as an appetizer or as a complement to salads and other dishes.

Preheat panini grill to high

2	7-inch (18 cm) pitas	2
1 tbsp	olive oil	15 mL
1/4 cup	hummus	50 mL
4 to 6	thin slices red onion	4 to 6
1/2 cup	diced seeded cucumber	125 mL
1/4 cup	sliced roasted red bell peppers	50 mL
1/4 cup	drained pitted kalamata olives, halved	50 mL
1/4 cup	diced seeded tomato	50 mL
1/4 cup	crumbled feta cheese	50 mL
Pinch	freshly ground black pepper	Pinch
Pinch	dried oregano	Pinch

1. Brush one side of each pita with oil. Place on a work surface, oiled side down, and spread hummus over half of each pita, dividing evenly and leaving a 1/2-inch (1 cm) border around the edges. Evenly layer onion to taste, cucumber, roasted peppers, olives, tomato and feta on top of hummus. Sprinkle with pepper and oregano. Fold pitas over filling, pressing gently to pack.

2. Place sandwiches in grill, close the top plate and cook until golden brown, 3 to 4 minutes. Serve immediately.

Sautéed Vegetable Panini

The meaty yet earthy flavor of portobello mushrooms makes a great foundation for red peppers and red onions, laced with smoked mozzarella.

Serves 2

Tips

You can identify portobello mushrooms by the dark gills beneath their caps. A mature portobello cap can be up to 6 inches (15 cm) in diameter.

Alfalfa sprouts will last in the refrigerator for only a few days before they become wilted.

Preheat panini grill to high

1 tbsp	olive oil	15 mL
2 cups	sliced portobello mushroom caps	500 mL
½ cup	sliced red bell pepper	125 mL
½ cup	sliced red onion	125 mL
2	4-inch (10 cm) focaccia, halved horizontally	2
1 tbsp	olive oil	15 mL
2 tbsp	Sun-Dried Tomato Mayonnaise (see recipe, page 236)	25 mL
2 oz	smoked mozzarella cheese, sliced	60 g
4	thin slices tomato	4
¼ cup	alfalfa sprouts	50 mL

1. In a large nonstick skillet, heat oil over medium heat. Add mushrooms, red pepper and onion; sauté until tender, 7 to 9 minutes. Remove from heat and let cool.

2. Place focaccia, cut side down, on a work surface and brush crusts with oil. Turn focaccia over and spread with mayonnaise. On bottom halves, evenly layer with mushroom mixture, mozzarella, tomato and alfalfa sprouts. Cover with top halves and press gently to pack.

3. Place sandwiches in grill, close the top plate and cook until golden brown, 3 to 4 minutes. Serve immediately.

Grilled Portobello Panini

Grilling the portobello mushrooms and onion gives this panini a wonderfully rich, sweet flavor. Smoked gouda is the perfect match to the grilled vegetables, which are enhanced even further by the peppery arugula.

Serves 2

Tip
Enjoy this panini with a full-bodied red wine.

Preheat panini grill to high

2	portobello mushrooms, stems and gills removed	2
½	small red onion, thinly sliced	½
2 tbsp	olive oil, divided	25 mL
Pinch	salt	Pinch
Pinch	freshly ground black pepper	Pinch
4	slices sourdough bread (½-inch/1 cm thick slices)	4
1 tbsp	basil pesto (store-bought or see recipe, page 245)	15 mL
1 tbsp	mayonnaise	15 mL
2 oz	smoked Gouda cheese, thinly sliced	60 g
½ cup	arugula	125 mL
¼ cup	thinly sliced drained oil-packed sun-dried tomatoes	50 mL
¼ cup	sliced roasted red bell peppers	50 mL

1. Brush both sides of the mushrooms and onion with 1 tbsp (15 mL) of the oil and sprinkle with salt and pepper. Arrange on bottom grill plate, close the top plate and grill until mushrooms are tender and grill-marked, 3 to 5 minutes. Remove, slice mushroom caps and separate onion rings, and keep warm. Wipe grill plates clean.

2. Brush one side of each bread slice with the remaining olive oil. Place on a work surface, oiled side down, and spread pesto over the bottom halves. Spread mayonnaise over the top halves. On bottom halves, evenly layer with grilled mushrooms and onion, Gouda, arugula, tomatoes and roasted peppers. Cover with top halves and press gently to pack.

3. Place sandwiches on grill, close the top plate and cook until golden brown, 3 to 4 minutes. Serve immediately.

Stir-Fried Mushroom and Mozzarella Panini

Sautéed cremini mushrooms, combined with creamy mozzarella cheese, make for a simple yet hearty panini.

Serves 2

Tips

Cremini mushrooms are immature portobello mushrooms; thus, they are sometimes known as baby bellas.

Bolillo rolls — one of the most popular breads in Mexico — are made with a basic dough similar to French baguette dough. The rolls have a crispy crust with a soft, chewy crumb. If you can't find them, you can substitute submarine rolls, sourdough rolls or hoagie rolls.

Preheat panini grill to high

2 tbsp	olive oil, divided	25 mL
1½ cups	sliced cremini (baby bella) mushrooms	375 mL
Pinch	salt	Pinch
Pinch	freshly ground black pepper	Pinch
Pinch	dried basil	Pinch
2	bolillo rolls, split	2
2 oz	mozzarella cheese, thinly sliced	60 g

1. In a nonstick skillet, heat 1 tbsp (15 mL) of the oil over medium-high heat. Add mushrooms, salt, pepper and basil; sauté until tender, 7 to 9 minutes. Remove from heat and keep warm.

2. Place rolls, cut side down, on a work surface and brush crusts with the remaining oil. Turn rolls over and, on bottom halves, evenly layer with mushroom mixture and mozzarella. Cover with top halves and press gently to pack.

3. Place sandwiches in grill, close the top plate and cook until golden brown, 3 to 4 minutes. Serve immediately.

Refried Bean Panini

This recipe is very easy to prepare, and you will love its flavor!

Serves 2

Tip

For a spicy panini, keep the ribs and seeds of the jalapeño, or use a hotter chile pepper, such as a habanero.

Preheat panini grill to high

2	8- or 10-inch (20 or 25 cm) flour tortillas	2
1 tsp	butter, melted	5 mL
½ cup	refried beans	125 mL
½ cup	shredded Cheddar cheese	125 mL
1	small avocado, thinly sliced	1
1	small jalapeño pepper, seeds and ribs removed, thinly sliced	1

1. Brush one side of each tortilla with butter. Place on a work surface, buttered side down, and spread refried beans over half of each tortilla, dividing evenly and leaving a ½-inch (1 cm) border around the edges. Sprinkle with cheese and evenly layer avocado and jalapeño on top of beans. Fold tortillas over filling, pressing gently to pack.

2. Place sandwiches in grill, close the top plate and cook until filling is hot and cheese is melted, 3 to 4 minutes. Cut each sandwich in half and serve immediately.

Open-Faced Tofu, Mushroom and Roasted Pepper Panini

Sautéed tofu, cremini mushrooms, roasted red peppers and mozzarella cheese make this healthy panini a winner. It's served open-faced, so don't forget your fork!

Serves 2

Tip

Tofu, which is sometimes fortified with calcium, comes in regular, low-fat and nonfat. Its texture is smooth and creamy, yet it's firm enough to slice. Tofu has a bland, slightly nutty flavor, but it has the amazing ability to take on the flavor of the food with which it is cooked. It can be sliced, diced or mashed and used in a variety of dishes, including soups, stir-fries, casseroles, salads, sandwiches, salad dressings and sauces. Tofu is very perishable and should be kept in the refrigerator for no more than a week. All tofu should be stored covered with water, which should be changed daily.

Preheat panini grill to high

2 tbsp	olive oil, divided	25 mL
1 cup	thinly sliced cremini (baby bella) mushrooms	250 mL
4 oz	firm tofu, drained, patted dry and cut into ½-inch (1 cm) cubes	125 g
½ cup	sliced roasted red bell peppers	125 mL
Pinch	salt	Pinch
Pinch	freshly ground black pepper	Pinch
1 tbsp	basil pesto (store-bought or see recipe, page 245)	15 mL
2	slices sourdough bread (½-inch/1 cm thick slices)	2
½ cup	marinara sauce	125 mL
½ cup	shredded mozzarella cheese	125 mL

1. In a nonstick skillet, heat 1 tbsp (15 mL) of the oil over medium–high heat. Add mushrooms and sauté until tender about 5 minutes. Add tofu, roasted peppers, salt and pepper; sauté until heated through, about 5 minutes. Stir in pesto and remove from heat.

2. Meanwhile, place bread slices on a work surface and brush both sides with the remaining olive oil. Place in grill, close the top plate and cook until toasted, with grill marks, 1 to 2 minutes. Remove from grill and return to work surface. Spread both slices with marinara sauce, evenly layer with tofu mixture and top with mozzarella.

3. Return assembled sandwiches to the grill, lower the top plate to within ½ inch (1 cm) of the filling and hold until cheese is melted, 1 to 2 minutes. Serve immediately, open-faced.

Fish and Seafood Panini

Tuna, Basil and Tomato Panini

Fresh tuna steaks are a wonderful panini ingredient. I added crisp bacon, but you could omit it if you want the flavor of the grilled tuna to be the focus.

Serves 2

Tip

If you're short on time, you can use plain mayonnaise instead of the basil mayonnaise.

Variation

Feel free to add cheese — mozzarella would be a good choice.

Preheat panini grill to high

2	tuna steaks (each 5 to 6 oz/150 to 175 g, about ¾ inch/2 cm thick)	2
2 tbsp	olive oil, divided	25 mL
Pinch	salt	Pinch
Pinch	freshly ground black pepper	Pinch
4	slices French bread (½-inch/1 cm thick slices)	4
3 tbsp	Basil Mayonnaise (see recipe, page 236)	45 mL
4	fresh basil leaves	4
4	thin slices tomato	4
4	slices bacon, cooked crisp	4
2	romaine lettuce leaves	2

1. Brush tuna with 1 tbsp (15 mL) of the oil and sprinkle with salt and pepper. Arrange on bottom grill plate, close the top plate and grill until seared on the outside and pink on the inside, 3 to 5 minutes. Transfer to a plate and keep warm. Wipe grill plates clean.

2. Brush one side of each bread slice with the remaining oil. Place on a work surface, oiled side down, and spread with mayonnaise. Place 1 tuna steak on each bottom half, then evenly layer with basil, tomato, bacon and lettuce. Cover with top halves and press gently to pack.

3. Place sandwiches in grill, close the top plate and cook until golden brown, 3 to 4 minutes. Serve immediately.

Carol's Tuna Melt

Tuna melts are a classic, and just about everyone makes some version of them, but I am using my dear friend Carol's recipe. Make sure to set the top plate of the panini grill so that it just touches the sandwich, as pressing can force out juices from the tuna mixture, creating soggy bread.

Serves 2

Tip
Cut calories and fat by using low-fat mayonnaise and nonstick cooking spray instead of butter.

Variation
Add the crunch of chopped pecans or crumbled potato chips for a unique texture and flavor.

Preheat panini grill to high

1	can (6 oz/170 g) water-packed tuna, drained and flaked	1
4	green onions, sliced	4
1	stalk celery, finely chopped	1
1 tbsp	mayonnaise	15 mL
Pinch	salt	Pinch
Pinch	freshly ground black pepper	Pinch
4	slices wheat bread (½-inch/1 cm thick slices)	4
1 tbsp	butter, melted	15 mL
½ cup	shredded Swiss cheese	125 mL

1. In a bowl, combine tuna, green onions, celery, mayonnaise, salt and pepper.

2. Brush one side of each bread slice with butter. Place two slices on a work surface, buttered side down, and evenly layer with tuna mixture ⋅ cheese. Cover with top halves, buttered and press gently to pack.

3. Place sandwiches in grill, cl⋅ that it barely touches th⋅ until golden brow⋅ immediately.

Marcia's Tuna and Swiss Panini

My dear friend and workout partner Marcia loves this flavor combination and offered it as a suggestion for panini. This recipe, packed with protein, is great with spreadable Swiss cheese, but it would work with Swiss cheese slices too.

Serves 2

Tip

Make sure to properly drain the tuna to keep the bread from getting soggy.

Variation

Pita bread is perfect for this recipe, but you could also try a hearty, high-fiber multigrain bread.

Preheat panini grill to high

1	can (6 oz/170 g) water-packed tuna (preferably albacore), drained	1
Pinch	salt	Pinch
Pinch	freshly ground black pepper	Pinch
2	5-inch (12.5 cm) pitas	2
1 tbsp	olive oil	15 mL
3 oz	Swiss-flavored spreadable cheese (such as Laughing Cow)	90 g
2	romaine lettuce leaves	2
½	orange bell pepper, thinly sliced	½

1. In a small bowl, combine tuna, salt and pepper.

2. Brush one side of each pita with oil. Place on a work surface, oiled side down, and spread with cheese. On one pita, evenly layer with tuna mixture, lettuce and orange pepper. Cover with remaining pita, oiled side up, and press gently to pack.

3. Place sandwich in grill, close the top plate and cook until golden brown, 3 to 4 minutes. Cut in half and serve immediately.

Tuna and Artichoke Panini

This flavor combination is great tossed in a salad and works just as well in a panini.

Serves 2

Tips

Niçoise olives are terrific, but kalamata, Greek or other brine-cured olives will be great too.

Drain the tuna and artichokes well to remove excess water; otherwise, you'll end up with soggy bread.

Preheat panini grill to high

1	can (6 oz/170 g) water-packed tuna (preferably albacore), drained	1
4	water-packed canned artichokes, drained	4
2 tbsp	chopped roasted red bell pepper	25 mL
2 tbsp	thinly sliced fresh basil	25 mL
2 tsp	chopped drained Niçoise olives	10 mL
1 tsp	drained capers	5 mL
2 tbsp	mayonnaise	25 mL
1 tbsp	freshly squeezed lemon juice	15 mL
Pinch	salt	Pinch
Pinch	freshly ground black pepper	Pinch
2	hoagie buns, split	2
1 tbsp	olive oil	15 mL
4	thin slices onion	4
4	thin slices tomato	4

1. In a bowl, combine tuna, artichokes, red pepper, basil, olives, capers, mayonnaise, lemon juice, salt and pepper.

2. Place rolls, cut side down, on a work surface and brush crusts with oil. Turn rolls over and, on bottom halves, evenly layer with tuna mixture, onion and tomato. Cover with top halves and press gently to pack.

3. Place sandwiches in grill, close the top plate and cook until golden brown, 3 to 4 minutes. Serve immediately.

Sardine and Balsamic Tomato Panini

Both my daddy and my grandfather love sardines on saltines, with yellow mustard. As a child, I craved this snack, thinking it was so grown-up (or perhaps it was the beginning of my culinary future). I did not put this recipe in the kids' chapter, for obvious reasons, but I hope you'll enjoy the ingredient lineup I paired with sardines.

Serves 2

Tips

These ingredients are also a perfect topping for toasted crostini, which I make in my panini grill.

Although I've mashed the sardines in this recipe, feel free use whole fillets.

Preheat panini grill to high

½ cup	chopped seeded tomatoes	125 mL
1 tsp	chopped fresh Italian (flat-leaf) parsley	5 mL
1 tsp	balsamic vinegar	5 mL
Pinch	salt	Pinch
Pinch	freshly ground black pepper	Pinch
4	slices Italian bread (½-inch/1 cm thick slices)	4
1 tbsp	olive oil	15 mL
2 tsp	mustard	10 mL
4	oil-packed canned sardines, drained and mashed	4
½ cup	freshly grated Parmesan cheese	125 mL

1. In a bowl, combine tomatoes, parsley, vinegar, salt and pepper.

2. Brush one side of each bread slice with oil. Place two slices on a work surface, oiled side down, and spread with mustard. Evenly layer with sardines, tomato mixture and cheese. Cover with top halves, oiled side up, and press gently to pack.

3. Place sandwiches in grill, close the top plate and cook until golden brown, 3 to 4 minutes. Serve immediately.

Salmon Croquette Panini

My pawpaw Luther always loved this family recipe. He'd put the leftover salmon between two slices of white bread for his lunch the next day. I kept the tradition of white bread, but used a dense sandwich roll to create the perfect panini.

Serves 2

Tips

As a child, I loved this sandwich with bottled ketchup, and guess what? Nothing has changed. My foodie friends cannot believe this, so to appease them and add a bit of elegance, I've used rémoulade as the spread in this recipe. Still, if, like me, you occasionally want to indulge your inner child, by all means substitute ketchup!

Store leftover salmon croquettes in an airtight container in the refrigerator for up to 4 days. Serve them with rémoulade, cocktail sauce or on top of a bed of greens as an entrée salad.

Preheat panini grill to high

1	can (15 oz/430 mL) pink salmon, drained, skin removed and mashed	1
1	egg, lightly beaten	1
3	green onions, thinly sliced	3
½ cup	finely chopped white onion	125 mL
¼ tsp	freshly ground black pepper	1 mL
⅔ cup	crushed saltine crackers (about 20)	150 mL
½ cup	vegetable oil	125 mL
2	sandwich rolls, split	2
1 tbsp	butter, melted	15 mL
¼ cup	Rémoulade (see recipe, page 241)	50 mL
4	thin slices tomato	4
2	thin slices red onion	2
2	lettuce leaves	2

1. In a bowl, gently combine salmon, egg, green onions, white onion and pepper. Divide mixture into 6 equal portions, shaping each into a ½-inch (1 cm) thick patty. Dredge patties in cracker crumbs, pressing to adhere. Discard any excess crumbs.

2. In a large skillet, heat oil over medium–high heat. Add patties and cook for 5 minutes on each side. Transfer to a plate lined with paper towels.

3. Brush both the cut and crust sides of rolls with butter. Place in grill, close the top plate and cook until toasted, with grill marks, 1 to 2 minutes. Remove from grill and place on a work surface, cut side up. Spread bottom halves with rémoulade. Place 1 salmon croquette on each bottom half, then evenly layer with tomato, onion and lettuce. Cover with top halves and press gently to pack. Serve immediately.

Salmon Panini with Wasabi Mayonnaise

Wasabi, the Japanese version of horseradish, accents this salmon panini with fire and flavor.

Serves 2

Tips

I like to dip this panini in soy sauce.

If you cannot find black sesame seeds, just use double the amount of regular sesame seeds.

Preheat panini grill to high

1	clove garlic, minced	1
1 tsp	minced gingerroot	5 mL
2 tbsp	soy sauce	25 mL
1 tbsp	rice vinegar	15 mL
2	salmon fillets (each 4 oz/125 g)	2
4	slices sourdough bread (½-inch/1 cm thick slices)	4
1 tbsp	olive oil	15 mL
3 tbsp	Wasabi Mayonnaise (see recipe, page 239)	45 mL
1 tsp	sesame seeds	5 mL
1 tsp	black sesame seeds	5 mL
1 cup	baby spinach leaves	250 mL
6	slices cucumber	6

1. In a small bowl, combine garlic, ginger, soy sauce and vinegar.

2. Using your hand, gently flatten salmon to an even thickness of about ½ inch (1 cm). Brush with garlic mixture. Arrange salmon on bottom grill plate, close the top plate and grill until salmon is opaque and grill-marked and flakes easily with a fork, 3 to 4 minutes. Transfer to a plate and keep warm. Wipe grill plates clean.

3. Brush one side of each bread slice with oil. Place on a work surface, oiled side down, and spread with mayonnaise. Place 1 salmon fillet on each bottom half. Combine sesame seeds and black sesame seeds; sprinkle evenly over salmon. Evenly layer with spinach and cucumber. Cover with top halves and press gently to pack.

4. Place sandwiches in grill, close the top plate and cook until golden brown, 3 to 4 minutes. Serve immediately.

Stacked Salmon Panini with Egg Salad and Olive Tapenade

Oh my, what a beautiful, elegant recipe this is, a great presentation for brunch. I served it at a seated luncheon and received rave reviews.

Serves 2

Variations

Take this recipe to the next level by substituting caviar for the olive tapenade.

I have made this recipe with poached eggs instead of egg salad.

Preheat panini grill to high

1	hard-boiled egg, chopped	1
1 tbsp	chopped fresh chives	15 mL
2 tbsp	sour cream	25 mL
Pinch	freshly ground black pepper	Pinch
2	sourdough English muffins, split	2
1 tbsp	butter, melted	15 mL
4 oz	smoked salmon, thinly sliced	125 g

Topping

1 tbsp	sour cream	15 mL
2 tsp	Olive Tapenade (see recipe, page 242)	10 mL
1 tbsp	chopped fresh chives	15 mL

1. In a small bowl, combine egg, chives, sour cream and black pepper. Set aside.

2. Brush both the cut and crust sides of muffins with butter. Place in grill, close the top plate and cook until toasted, with grill marks, 1 to 2 minutes. Remove from grill and place on a work surface, cut side up. On bottom halves, evenly layer with smoked salmon and egg salad.

3. Place sandwiches on plates, dollop with sour cream and tapenade, and sprinkle with chives. Serve immediately with grilled muffin top.

Smoked Salmon Panini with Olive Cream Cheese

Smoked salmon is wonderful paired with kalamata olives in a blend of cream cheese, goat cheese and fresh chives.

Serves 2

Tip

The cream cheese mixture is also great as a spread for crackers or on its own in a panini.

Variation

For a different texture, use your favorite bagel instead of ciabatta rolls. This variation would be perfect for brunch.

Preheat panini grill to high

6 tbsp	cream cheese, softened	90 mL
2 oz	goat cheese, softened	60 g
2 tbsp	chopped fresh chives	25 mL
1 tbsp	finely chopped drained kalamata olives	15 mL
¼ tsp	salt	1 mL
¼ tsp	freshly ground black pepper	1 mL
½ tsp	freshly squeezed lemon juice	2 mL
2	ciabatta rolls, split	2
1 tbsp	olive oil	15 mL
4 oz	smoked salmon, thinly sliced	125 g
1 cup	arugula	250 mL
4	thin slices red onion	4

1. In a bowl, combine cream cheese, goat cheese, chives, olives, salt, pepper and lemon juice.

2. Place rolls, cut side down, on a work surface and brush crusts with oil. Turn rolls over and spread with cream cheese mixture. On bottom halves, evenly layer with salmon, arugula and red onion. Cover with top halves and press gently to pack.

3. Place sandwiches in grill, close the top plate and cook until golden brown, 3 to 4 minutes. Serve immediately.

Norwegian Smoked Salmon Panini

Mascarpone is a creamy counterpoint to this panini of delicate smoked salmon, capers, tomato and chives.

Serves 2

Tips

Norwegian smoked salmon is an oilier fish, cold-smoked and mildly salted, with just a hint of hardwood smoke flavor. Because it is moderately expensive, smoked salmon is considered a delicacy in many parts of the world.

If you cannot find mascarpone cheese, use softened cream cheese.

Preheat panini grill to high

2	4-inch (10 cm) focaccia, halved horizontally	2
1 tbsp	olive oil	15 mL
1/4 cup	mascarpone cheese	50 mL
2 tbsp	drained capers	25 mL
4 oz	Norwegian smoked salmon, thinly sliced	125 g
1	plum (Roma) tomato, thinly sliced	1
1 tbsp	chopped fresh chives	15 mL
2	lemon wedges	2

1. Place focaccia, cut side down, on a work surface and brush crusts with oil. Turn focaccia over, spread bottom halves with cheese and sprinkle with capers. Evenly layer with salmon and tomato. Sprinkle with chives and squeeze lemon juice over top. Cover with top halves and press gently to pack.

2. Place sandwiches in grill, close the top plate and cook until golden brown, 3 to 4 minutes. Serve immediately.

Fried Catfish Panini

When I was growing up, my family always served fried fish on meatless Fridays, so I've seen catfish prepared in more ways than you can imagine. But the delicate fried fish prepared by my friends Tom and Lisa Perini is the best of the best. At Perini Steakhouse, in Buffalo Gap, Texas, they serve up a mound of fried fish that truly melts in your mouth. I've tried to match it in this panini recipe.

Serves 2

Tip

For perfectly cooked fish, you must heat the oil to the proper temperature. Fried fish is done when it floats on top of the oil.

Preheat panini grill to high
Candy/deep-fry thermometer

3 cups	vegetable oil (approx.)	750 mL
1	egg	1
¾ cup	milk	175 mL
2 tsp	seasoning salt	10 mL
½ tsp	freshly ground white pepper	2 mL
1 cup	yellow cornmeal	250 mL
2 tbsp	all-purpose flour	25 mL
½ tsp	salt	2 mL
½ tsp	cayenne pepper	2 mL
¼ tsp	freshly ground black pepper	1 mL
Pinch	onion powder	Pinch
Pinch	garlic powder	Pinch
2	skinless catfish fillets (each 6 oz/175 g), halved lengthwise	2
2	submarine rolls, split	2
1 tbsp	butter, melted	15 mL
½ cup	Fay's Tartar Sauce (see recipe, page 240)	125 mL
2	lettuce leaves	2
4	thin slices tomato	4

1. In a deep, heavy skillet, heat about 2 inches (5 cm) of oil over high heat until it registers 375°F (190°C) on thermometer, about 10 minutes.

2. Meanwhile, in a shallow bowl, whisk together egg, milk, seasoning salt and white pepper; set aside.

Tip

Enjoy this recipe while entertaining friends or family by following Steps 1 through 4 and adjusting the amount of fish and the coating ingredients according to the number of guests you have.

3. On a large plate, combine cornmeal, flour, salt, cayenne, black pepper, onion powder and garlic powder.

4. Dip catfish in egg mixture, turning to coat both sides, then coat with seasoned cornmeal. Shake excess cornmeal from the fish and discard any excess cornmeal and egg mixtures. Carefully transfer fish to the hot oil and fry, turning if necessary, until fish floats, about 6 minutes. Using a slotted spoon, transfer to a plate lined with paper towels and keep warm.

5. Brush both the cut and crust sides of rolls with butter. Place in grill, close the top plate and cook until toasted, with grill marks, 1 to 2 minutes. Remove from grill and place on a work surface, cut side up. Spread bottom halves with tartar sauce. Place 1 fried fish fillet on each bottom half, then evenly layer with lettuce and tomato. Cover with top halves and press gently to pack. Serve immediately.

Blackened Tilapia Panini

Blackened tilapia creates remarkable flavor in this panini, but if you prefer, you could simply grill or pan-fry it with salt, pepper and a splash of lemon juice. Either way, the flavor is enhanced by fresh tomato, jalapeño mayonnaise and melted provolone.

Serves 2

Tips

Serve with a side of couscous and marinated cucumbers.

Instead of pan-frying the tilapia, try grilling it outdoors for wonderful flavor.

Preheat panini grill to high
Cast-iron skillet

1 tsp	paprika	5 mL
½ tsp	dry mustard	2 mL
¼ tsp	cayenne pepper	1 mL
¼ tsp	ground cumin	1 mL
¼ tsp	freshly ground black pepper	1 mL
¼ tsp	garlic powder	1 mL
¼ tsp	dried thyme	1 mL
¼ tsp	salt	1 mL
¼ cup	butter, melted	50 mL
2	skinless tilapia fillets (each 4 oz/125 g)	2
4	slices Italian bread (½-inch/1 cm thick slices)	4
1 tbsp	olive oil	15 mL
¼ cup	Jalapeño Mayonnaise (see recipe, page 238)	50 mL
2 oz	provolone cheese, thinly sliced	60 g
1	plum (Roma) tomato, thinly sliced	1

1. Heat cast-iron skillet over high heat until hot, about 10 minutes.

2. Meanwhile, in a small bowl, combine paprika, mustard, cayenne, cumin, black pepper, garlic powder, thyme and salt.

3. Place butter in a shallow dish. Dip tilapia in butter, turning to coat both sides. Sprinkle both sides with spice mixture and pat onto fillets.

Tips

Tilapia has a sweet, mild flavor and a firm texture that makes it suitable for all types of cooking methods, including grilling and pan-frying.

For leftovers, blacken extra tilapia fillets and serve over your favorite salad recipe.

4. Place fillets in hot pan and carefully drizzle about 1 tsp (5 mL) butter over each fillet. Cook until fish appears charred, about 2 minutes. Turn fillets, spoon 1 tsp (5 mL) butter over each, and cook until charred. Transfer to a plate.

5. Brush one side of each bread slice with oil. Place on a work surface, oiled side down, and spread with mayonnaise. Place 1 tilapia fillet on each bottom half, then evenly layer with cheese and tomato. Cover with top halves and press gently to pack.

6. Place sandwiches in grill, close the top plate and cook until golden brown, 3 to 4 minutes. Serve immediately.

Mediterranean Swordfish Panini

This beautiful panini boasts firm swordfish steaks in a marinade that evokes the Mediterranean. Grill extra and toss it in pasta with bell peppers, tomato and arugula.

Serves 2

Tip

Swordfish is available fresh from late spring to early fall, but can be found frozen year-round. Sold in either steaks or chunks, swordfish is very firm, which is great for grilling.

2 tbsp	freshly squeezed lemon juice	25 mL
2 tbsp	freshly squeezed orange juice	25 mL
2 tbsp	freshly squeezed lime juice	25 mL
Pinch	dried oregano	Pinch
Pinch	dried thyme	Pinch
Pinch	dried basil	Pinch
Pinch	garlic powder	Pinch
Pinch	salt	Pinch
Pinch	freshly ground black pepper	Pinch
2	swordfish fillets (each 4 oz/125 g, ¾ to 1 inch/2 to 2.5 cm thick)	2
2 tbsp	olive oil, divided	25 mL
4	slices French bread (½-inch/1 cm thick slices)	4
¼ cup	aïoli (store-bought or see recipe, page 240)	50 mL
1	plum (Roma) tomato, thinly sliced	1
½	red bell pepper, thinly sliced	½
½	yellow bell pepper, thinly sliced	½
½ cup	arugula	125 mL

1. In a large, sealable plastic bag, combine lemon juice, orange juice, lime juice, oregano, thyme, basil, garlic powder, salt and pepper. Add swordfish, seal and marinate in the refrigerator for 15 to 30 minutes. Remove swordfish and discard marinade.

2. Preheat panini grill to high. Brush both sides of swordfish with 1 tbsp (15 mL) of the oil and arrange on bottom grill plate. Close the top plate and grill until swordfish is opaque and flakes easily with a fork, 3 to 5 minutes. Transfer to a plate and keep warm. Wipe grill plates clean.

Tips

Be careful not to marinate the fish for longer than is indicated in the recipe, or it will be cooked by the citric acid in the lemon juice.

Serve with a bowl of tomato basil soup drizzled with a swirl of crème fraîche.

3. Brush one side of each bread slice with the remaining oil. Place on a work surface, oiled side down, and spread with aïoli. Place 1 swordfish fillet on each bottom half, then evenly layer with tomato, red pepper, yellow pepper and arugula. Cover with top halves and press gently to pack.

4. Place sandwiches in grill, close the top plate and cook until golden brown, 3 to 4 minutes. Serve immediately.

Oyster Po' Boy

When I was growing up, delicate raw oysters were much-loved fare on my family's menu, but I preferred it when my mom fried the oysters in a crispy coating and served them in a sandwich slathered with her homemade tartar sauce.

Serves 2

Tips

If you prefer, substitute shredded cabbage or drained coleslaw for the iceberg lettuce.

Serve with lemon wedges for a squirt of freshness.

Preheat panini grill to high
Candy/deep-fry thermometer

3 cups	vegetable oil (approx.)	750 mL
1	egg	1
¼ cup	milk	50 mL
1 tsp	salt, divided	5 mL
¾ cup	yellow cornmeal	175 mL
¼ cup	white cornmeal	50 mL
¼ tsp	freshly ground black pepper	1 mL
¼ tsp	cayenne pepper	1 mL
12	shucked oysters (see box, at right), drained and patted dry	12
2	6-inch (15 cm) French baguettes, split	2
1 tbsp	butter, melted	15 mL
½ cup	Fay's Tartar Sauce (see recipe, page 240)	125 mL
½ cup	shredded iceberg lettuce	125 mL

1. In a deep, heavy skillet, heat about 2 inches (5 cm) of oil over high heat until it registers 375°F (190°C) on thermometer, about 10 minutes.

2. Meanwhile, in a shallow bowl, whisk together egg, milk, and ½ tsp (5 mL) of the salt; set aside.

3. In a large, sealable plastic bag, combine yellow cornmeal, white cornmeal, the remaining salt, black pepper and cayenne.

Tips

Oysters should be eaten as fresh as possible. If their shells are not tightly shut, don't eat them!

I enjoy this panini with a seafood cocktail sauce, which can be found near the fresh seafood in your local supermarket or in the condiment section.

4. Working in batches, add oysters to egg mixture, then lift out, letting excess drip off. Add to the cornmeal mixture, seal and shake to coat well. Shake excess cornmeal from the oysters and discard any excess cornmeal and egg mixtures. Carefully transfer oysters to the hot oil and fry, turning once, until golden and cooked through, 1 to 2 minutes. Using a slotted spoon, transfer to a plate lined with paper towels and keep warm. Repeat with the remaining oysters, returning the oil to 375°F (190°C) between each batch.

5. Brush both the cut and crust sides of baguettes with butter. Place in grill, close the top plate and cook until toasted, with grill marks, 1 to 2 minutes. Remove from grill and place on a work surface, cut side up. Spread bottom halves with tartar sauce and evenly layer with oysters and lettuce. Cover with top halves and press gently to pack. Serve immediately.

To shuck oysters

Hold the oyster firmly in one hand, an oyster knife in the other. Slip the knife blade between the top and bottom shell, right by the hinge on the back. Be careful — the shell ridges are sharp! Run the knife all the way around the oyster until you get to the other side. Using a twisting motion, pry the top and bottom shells apart. Cut the oyster free from its shell (it will be connected by a tough knob on the underside).

Shrimp Po' Boy

My childhood memories include going deep-sea fishing off the Texas coast and catching loads of shrimp and crab. In the evening, I'd have a lot of fun watching my daddy and Uncle Jim fry shrimp. We'd have wonderful shrimp sandwiches, just like these, the next day.

Serves 2

Tip

While you have the oil heated, why not fry hand-cut potatoes to serve with this recipe?

Preheat panini grill to high
Candy/deep-fry thermometer

3 cups	vegetable oil (approx.)	750 mL
1	egg	1
¼ cup	buttermilk	50 mL
2 tsp	salt, divided	10 mL
2 cups	white cornmeal	500 mL
½ tsp	freshly ground black pepper	2 mL
½ tsp	cayenne pepper	2 mL
8 oz	large shrimp, peeled and deveined	250 g
2	6-inch (15 cm) French baguettes, split	2
1 tbsp	butter, melted	15 mL
½ cup	Rémoulade (see recipe, page 241)	125 mL
½ cup	shredded iceberg lettuce	125 mL

1. In a deep, heavy skillet, heat about 2 inches (5 cm) of oil over high heat until it registers 375°F (190°C) on thermometer, about 10 minutes.

2. Meanwhile, in a shallow bowl, whisk together egg, buttermilk, and 1 tsp (5 mL) of the salt; set aside.

3. In a large, sealable plastic bag, combine cornmeal, the remaining salt, black pepper and cayenne.

Tips

I love the coating on the shrimp in this recipe, but you could also prepare a tempura batter, which incorporates leavening agents such as baking soda and baking powder, for a light and fluffy shrimp coating.

To save valuable prep time, purchase peeled and deveined shrimp.

4. Working in batches, add shrimp to egg mixture, then lift out, letting excess drip off. Add to the cornmeal mixture, seal and shake to coat well. Shake excess cornmeal from the shrimp and discard any excess cornmeal and egg mixtures. Carefully transfer shrimp to the hot oil and fry, turning once, until golden and cooked through, 1 to 2 minutes. Using a slotted spoon, transfer to a plate lined with paper towels and keep warm. Repeat with the remaining shrimp, returning the oil to 375°F (190°C) between each batch.

5. Brush both the cut and crust sides of baguettes with butter. Place in grill, close the top plate and cook until toasted, with grill marks, 1 to 2 minutes. Remove from grill and place on a work surface, cut side up. Spread bottom halves with rémoulade and evenly layer with shrimp and lettuce. Cover with top halves and press gently to pack. Serve immediately.

Shrimp counts

I am often asked how many shrimp there are per pound (500 g) in each size category. Here is a handy chart that will assist you when you're purchasing shrimp:

Size	Number of shrimp per 1 lb (500 g)
Small	45+
Medium	37 to 40
Large	26 to 29
Jumbo	15 to 18
Colossal	about 11

Shrimp Club Panini

To me, this is the perfect recipe, with the ideal mix of ingredients. Make sure you have extra napkins ready before you bite into this sandwich — you will need them!

Serves 2

Tips

If you have leftover grilled shrimp from a cookout, they would be wonderful in this recipe.

Remove the flesh of an avocado by cutting it in half lengthwise. Twist it open, leaving the pit on one side. Gently strike the pit with a large, sharp knife (I use my French knife) and twist again to remove the pit. Using a large soup spoon, scoop the flesh from the skin and slice it. Avocado flesh browns easily once it is sliced; to keep browning to a minimum, sprinkle it with lime or lemon juice.

Variation

Try using freshly baked, thickly sliced sourdough bread — what a treat!

Preheat panini grill to high

1	tomato, thinly sliced	1
1/4 tsp	salt	1 mL
1/4 tsp	freshly ground black pepper	1 mL
2	Italian rolls, split	2
1 tbsp	olive oil	15 mL
1/4 cup	mayonnaise	50 mL
8 oz	medium shrimp, cooked and halved lengthwise	250 g
2 oz	Swiss cheese, thinly sliced	60 g
4	slices bacon, cooked crisp	4
1	large avocado, sliced	1

1. Sprinkle tomato slices evenly with salt and pepper; set aside.

2. Place rolls, cut side down, on a work surface and brush crusts with oil. Turn rolls over and spread with mayonnaise. On bottom halves, evenly layer with shrimp, cheese, bacon, avocado and seasoned tomato. Cover with top halves and press gently to pack.

3. Place sandwiches in grill, close the top plate and cook until golden brown, 3 to 4 minutes. Serve immediately.

Shrimp, Spinach and Gouda Panini

One of my favorite pasta dishes includes shrimp sautéed in garlicky, lemony olive oil, finished with a quick wilt of baby spinach and topped with shredded Gouda. So I turned it into a panini.

Serves 2

Variations

Try adding a sprinkle of toasted pine nuts or a smear of pesto.

Substitute 2 oz (60 g) shaved Parmesan for the Gouda, or use both.

Preheat panini grill to high

1	clove garlic, minced	1
2 tbsp	olive oil, divided	25 mL
1 tbsp	freshly squeezed lemon juice	15 mL
Pinch	salt	Pinch
Pinch	freshly ground black pepper	Pinch
4 oz	medium shrimp, peeled, deveined and butterflied	125 g
4	slices sourdough bread (½-inch/1 cm thick slices)	4
4 oz	Gouda cheese, thinly sliced	125 g
1 cup	baby spinach leaves	250 mL

1. In a bowl, combine garlic, 1 tbsp (15 mL) of the oil, lemon juice, salt and pepper. Add shrimp and toss to coat. Arrange shrimp on bottom grill plate, close the top plate and grill until pink and opaque, 2 to 3 minutes. Transfer to a plate and keep warm. Wipe grill plates clean.

2. Brush one side of each bread slice with the remaining oil. Place on a work surface, oiled side down, and evenly layer with cheese. On bottom halves, evenly layer with spinach and shrimp. Cover with top halves and press gently to pack.

3. Place sandwiches in grill, close the top plate and cook until golden brown, 3 to 4 minutes. Serve immediately.

Soft-Shell Crab Sandwiches

I was fortunate enough to study culinary arts at Johnson and Wales University in Charleston, South Carolina, where soft-shell crab is extremely popular. I quickly learned that this delicacy can be prepared in a number of ways. My choice is to fry it and put it in panini.

Serves 2

Tips

Be careful not to press the top plate down with too much force.

Hamburger buns are the perfect size and shape for the crab.

I love this sandwich with cocktail sauce spiked with Worcestershire sauce, either as a dip or spread on the bread.

Preheat panini grill to high

¼ cup	white cornmeal	50 mL
¼ cup	all-purpose flour	50 mL
1 tbsp	Cajun seasoning (such as Old Bay)	15 mL
1 tsp	freshly ground black pepper	5 mL
2	soft-shell crabs, dressed (see box, at right)	2
2 tbsp	butter, melted	25 mL
¼ cup	vegetable oil	50 mL
2	sandwich rolls or hamburger buns, split	2
1 tbsp	butter, melted	15 mL
½ cup	Fay's Tartar Sauce (see recipe, page 240)	125 mL
4	thin slices tomato	4
2	thin slices onion	2
2	large red-tipped lettuce leaves	2

1. In a bowl, combine cornmeal, flour, Cajun seasoning and pepper. Brush crabs with melted butter. Dredge crabs in cornmeal mixture, shaking off excess. Discard any excess butter and cornmeal mixture.

2. In a nonstick skillet, heat oil over medium–high heat. Add crabs and cook, turning once, until crisp and golden brown on both sides, 2 to 3 minutes per side. Transfer to a plate lined with paper towels.

Tip

Soft-shell crabs are actually blue crabs that have shed their shells and are preparing to grow new ones. Live soft-shell crabs are very popular and are flown all over the world when in season. You can find them on restaurant menus year-round; out of season, they will have been frozen in the molting stage.

3. Brush both the cut and crust sides of rolls with butter. Place in grill, close the top plate and cook until toasted, with grill marks, 1 to 2 minutes. Remove from grill and place on a work surface, cut side up. Spread bottom halves with tartar sauce. Place 1 fried crab on each bottom half, then evenly layer with tomato, onion and lettuce. Cover with top halves and press gently to pack. Serve immediately.

To dress soft-shell crabs

Hold a crab in one hand and, using a sharp knife, cut off the front of the crab, starting from about ½ inch (1 cm) behind the eyes and mouth. Remove the contents of the sac located behind the cut just made. Lift both pointed ends of the crab's outer shell, and remove and discard the gills. Turn the crab over and remove the apron, or small flap. Rinse and pat dry.

Lobster Fontina Panini

Many years ago, I traveled to Paradise Island, in the Bahamas, and dined in a tiny French restaurant, where I had the most amazing Lobster Newberg, topped with fontina cheese. The memory of this meal, my all-time favorite, inspired me to create this recipe.

Serves 2

Tip
I enjoy this recipe with a glass of chilled white wine — it truly doesn't get any better.

Variation
Substitute grilled shrimp or scallops for the lobster.

Preheat panini grill to high

2	ciabatta rolls, split	2
1 tbsp	butter, melted	15 mL
3 oz	fontina cheese, thinly sliced	90 g
1	lobster tail (6 to 8 oz/175 to 250 g), steamed, removed from shell and sliced	1
½ cup	baby spinach leaves	125 mL
½ cup	Caramelized Onions (see recipe, page 248)	125 mL

1. Place rolls, cut side down, on a work surface and brush crusts with butter. Turn rolls over and evenly layer with cheese. On bottom halves, evenly layer with lobster, spinach and caramelized onions. Cover with top halves and press gently to pack.

2. Place sandwiches in grill, close the top plate and cook until golden brown, 3 to 4 minutes. Serve immediately.

Chicken and Turkey Panini

continued, next page…

Chicken Barbecue Panini

Barbecue sauce is such a nice addition to this chicken panini, especially combined with red onion, avocado and fresh tomato.

Serves 2

Tips

Make sure you have lots of napkins nearby when serving this tasty panini.

Serve with your favorite potato salad and/or coleslaw.

Variation

Omit the avocado and tomato and add crunchy dill pickle slices.

Preheat panini grill to high

4	slices French bread (½-inch/1 cm thick slices)	4
1 tbsp	butter, melted	15 mL
4 oz	grilled chicken breast, thinly sliced	125 g
2 oz	provolone cheese, thinly sliced	60 g
½ cup	barbecue sauce (store-bought or see recipe, page 245)	125 mL
6	thin slices red onion	6
1	small avocado, sliced	1
1	small plum (Roma) tomato, thinly sliced	1

1. Brush one side of each bread slice with butter. Place on a work surface, buttered sides down. On bottom halves, evenly layer with chicken and cheese; drizzle with barbecue sauce. Evenly layer with onion, avocado and tomato. Cover with top halves and press gently to pack.

2. Place sandwiches in grill, close the top plate and cook until golden brown, 3 to 4 minutes. Serve immediately.

Chicken Pesto Panini

This is a very popular flavor combination: fragrant pesto, roasted chicken, sun-dried tomatoes, spinach and red onion, with a melting of provolone.

Serves 2

Tip

Make sure to drain the sun-dried tomatoes and pat them dry with a paper towel; otherwise, your bread may end up soggy.

Variations

For extra crunch and nutrition, add slices of red, yellow, green or orange bell peppers.

For a more intense flavor, replace the spinach with basil leaves.

Preheat panini grill to high

2	Italian rolls, split	2
1 tbsp	butter, melted	15 mL
¼ cup	basil pesto (store-bought or see recipe, page 245)	50 mL
2 oz	roasted chicken breast, thinly sliced	60 g
2 oz	provolone cheese, thinly sliced	60 g
½ cup	baby spinach leaves	125 mL
1 tbsp	chopped drained oil-packed sun-dried tomatoes	15 mL
4	thin slices red onion	4

1. Place rolls, cut side down, on a work surface and brush crusts with butter. Turn rolls over and spread with pesto. On bottom halves, evenly layer with chicken, cheese, spinach, sun-dried tomatoes and red onion. Cover with top halves and press gently to pack.

2. Place sandwiches in grill, close the top plate and cook until golden brown, 3 to 4 minutes. Serve immediately.

Southwest Chicken Panini

Flavors of the Southwest, with the added twist of peppery arugula, make this panini a true winner.

Serves 2

Tip
You can find sliced roasted chicken breast at your local deli. In a pinch, use grilled or rotisserie chicken breast.

Variation
Need more iron in your diet? Substitute spinach for the arugula.

Preheat panini grill to high

2	ciabatta rolls, split	2
1 tbsp	olive oil	15 mL
2 tbsp	Chipotle Mayonnaise (see recipe, page 237)	25 mL
4 oz	roasted chicken breast, thinly sliced	125 g
2 oz	pepper Jack cheese, thinly sliced	60 g
½ cup	arugula	125 mL
4	thin slices tomato	4
4	thin slices red onion	4
Pinch	salt	Pinch
Pinch	freshly ground black pepper	Pinch

1. Place rolls, cut side down, on a work surface and brush crusts with oil. Turn rolls over and spread with mayonnaise. On bottom halves, evenly layer with chicken, cheese, arugula, tomato and onion. Sprinkle with salt and pepper. Cover with top halves and press gently to pack.

2. Place sandwiches in grill, close the top plate and cook until golden brown, 3 to 4 minutes. Serve immediately.

Grilled Chicken and Tomatillo Quesadillas

This recipe is from my good friend Dianna Barrios Trevino, who is the owner of two family-owned Mexican restaurants in the San Antonio area: Los Barrios and La Hacienda De Los Barrios. It boasts many fresh ingredients that are popular in Mexican cuisine.

Serves 2

Variation

Substitute 3 tbsp (45 mL) fresh pico de gallo for the salsa and red onion. Use a favorite recipe, or look for it in the produce section of your supermarket.

Preheat panini grill to high

¾ cup	diced grilled chicken breast	175 mL
¼ cup	Tomatillo Sauce (see recipe, page 247)	50 mL
¼ cup	canned black beans, drained and rinsed	50 mL
¼ cup	frozen corn kernels, thawed	50 mL
¼ cup	diced tomato	50 mL
2 tbsp	finely chopped red onion	25 mL
1 tbsp	chopped fresh cilantro	15 mL
1 tbsp	sour cream	15 mL
1 tbsp	salsa	15 mL
2	8- to 10-inch (20 to 25 cm) flour tortillas	2
2 tsp	butter, melted	10 mL
½ cup	shredded Monterey Jack cheese	125 mL
	Thinly sliced avocado	

1. In a bowl, combine chicken, tomatillo sauce, beans, corn, tomato, onion, cilantro, sour cream and salsa.

2. Brush one side of each tortilla with butter. Place on a work surface, buttered side down, and spread chicken mixture over half of each tortilla, dividing evenly and leaving a ½-inch (1 cm) border around the edges. Sprinkle each with half the cheese. Fold tortillas over filling, pressing gently to pack.

3. Place sandwiches in grill, close the top plate and cook until filling is hot and cheese is melted, 3 to 4 minutes. Cut each sandwich in half and serve immediately, with avocado slices.

Chicken BLT Panini

This BLT goes beyond the typical bacon, lettuce and tomato, adding thin slices of roasted chicken, avocado, basil and aïoli for a gourmet twist on a classic sandwich.

Serves 2

Tip

If you don't have time to make aïoli, and can't find it in the grocery store, use mayonnaise.

Variation

Substitute shaved ham for the chicken for an all-pork version.

Preheat panini grill to high

2	ciabatta rolls, split	2
1 tbsp	olive oil	15 mL
¼ cup	aïoli (store-bought or see recipe, page 240)	50 mL
4 oz	roasted chicken breast, thinly sliced	125 g
4	slices thick-cut bacon, cooked crisp	4
2	romaine lettuce leaves	2
1	small avocado, thinly sliced	1
1	plum (Roma) tomato, thinly sliced	1
1 tbsp	thinly sliced fresh basil	15 mL

1. Place rolls, cut side down, on a work surface and brush crusts with oil. Turn rolls over and spread with aïoli. On bottom halves, evenly layer with chicken, bacon, lettuce, avocado and tomato. Sprinkle with basil. Cover with top halves and press gently to pack.

2. Place sandwiches in grill, close the top plate and cook until golden brown, 3 to 4 minutes. Serve immediately.

Chicken Caesar Panini

One of my favorite salads is the grilled chicken Caesar, so I made it into a panini!

Serves 2

Variation

Just as you would for a Caesar salad, substitute 8 oz (250 g) grilled shrimp for the chicken.

1	clove garlic, crushed	1
4 tbsp	olive oil, divided	60 mL
1 tbsp	freshly squeezed lemon juice	15 mL
½ tsp	hot pepper sauce (such as Tabasco)	2 mL
1 tsp	anchovy paste	5 mL
2	boneless skinless chicken breasts (each about 4 oz/125 g)	2
2	4-inch (10 cm) focaccia, halved horizontally	2
2	romaine lettuce leaves	2
½ cup	shaved Parmesan cheese	125 mL
Pinch	freshly ground black pepper	Pinch

1. In a large, sealable plastic bag, combine garlic, 3 tbsp (45 mL) of the oil, lemon juice, hot pepper sauce and anchovy paste. Remove 2 tbsp (25 mL) and set aside. Add chicken to the bag, seal and refrigerate for 1 to 2 hours. Remove chicken and discard marinade.

2. Preheat panini grill to high. Arrange chicken on bottom grill plate, close the top plate and grill until chicken is no longer pink inside, about 5 minutes. Transfer to a plate and keep warm. Wipe grill plates clean.

3. Place focaccia, cut side down, on a work surface and brush crusts with the remaining oil. Turn focaccia over and brush with the reserved marinade. On bottom halves, evenly layer with chicken, lettuce and cheese. Sprinkle with pepper. Cover with top halves and press gently to pack.

4. Place sandwiches in grill, close the top plate and cook until golden brown, 3 to 4 minutes. Serve immediately.

Grilled Chicken, Spinach, Red Pepper and Pepper Jack Panini

This recipe, loaded with flavor, is such an all-around beautiful masterpiece, it made the cover!

Serves 2

Variations

Turkey is a great substitute for the chicken. Look for flavored deli–sliced turkey, such as peppered turkey or Sausalito.

I sometimes like to use a mix of fresh red, green and yellow bell peppers in place of the roasted pepper.

Preheat panini grill to high

2	boneless skinless chicken breasts (each about 4 oz/125 g), pounded to ½-inch (1 cm) thick	2
Pinch	salt	Pinch
Pinch	freshly ground black pepper	Pinch
2	ciabatta rolls, split	2
1 tbsp	olive oil	15 mL
2 oz	pepper Jack cheese, sliced	60 g
½ cup	baby spinach leaves	125 mL
¼ cup	sliced roasted red bell pepper	50 mL

1. Sprinkle chicken with salt and pepper. Arrange on bottom grill plate, close the top plate and grill until chicken is no longer pink inside, about 5 minutes. Transfer to a plate and keep warm. Wipe grill plates clean.

2. Place rolls, cut side down, on a work surface and brush crusts with oil. Turn rolls over and, on bottom halves, evenly layer with grilled chicken, cheese, spinach and roasted pepper. Cover with top halves and press gently to pack.

3. Place sandwiches in grill, close the top plate and cook until golden brown, 3 to 4 minutes. Serve immediately.

Chicken, Spinach and Fontina Panini

I love how fontina cheese melts, especially in this panini. The flavor of the melted cheese is such a wonderful pairing with the chicken, spinach and sweet onion slices. I know you will enjoy this succulent sandwich.

Serves 2

Variations

Chopped toasted pecans are great paired with these ingredients. For convenience, purchase prechopped pecans. You'll pay a bit more, but the time saved is priceless.

Boston, or butter, lettuce is a great substitute for spinach.

Preheat panini grill to high

4	slices Italian bread (½-inch/1 cm thick slices)	4
1 tbsp	olive oil	15 mL
1 tbsp	mayonnaise	15 mL
1 tbsp	Dijon mustard	15 mL
2 oz	roasted chicken breast, thinly sliced	60 g
2 oz	fontina cheese, thinly sliced	60 g
8	large spinach leaves, trimmed	8
2	thin slices sweet onion	2

1. Brush one side of each bread slice with oil. Place on a work surface, oiled side down, and spread mayonnaise over bottom halves. Spread mustard over top halves. On bottom halves, evenly layer with chicken, cheese, spinach and onion. Cover with top halves and press gently to pack.

2. Place sandwiches in grill, close the top plate and cook until golden brown, 3 to 4 minutes. Serve immediately.

Grilled Chicken, Mozzarella and Pepperoni Panini

This chicken panini features traditional Italian ingredients such as mozzarella, pepperoni and tomato, but the arugula gives it a peppery twist.

Serves 2

Tip

Before adding the top half of the ciabatta rolls, sprinkle the filling with a good-quality balsamic vinegar for added flavor.

Preheat panini grill to high

2	ciabatta rolls, split	2
1 tbsp	olive oil	15 mL
4 oz	cooked chicken breast, sliced	125 g
2 oz	pepperoni, thinly sliced	60 g
1 cup	arugula	250 mL
½ cup	shredded mozzarella cheese	125 mL
6	slices plum (Roma) tomato	6

1. Place rolls, cut side down, on a work surface and brush crusts with oil. Turn rolls over and, on bottom halves, evenly layer with chicken, pepperoni, arugula, cheese and tomato. Cover with top halves and press gently to pack.

2. Place sandwiches in grill, close the top plate and cook until golden brown, 3 to 4 minutes. Serve immediately.

Blue Cheese, Chicken and Apple Panini

Roasted chicken breast, the sweet and tangy flavor of honey mustard, crisp Granny Smith apple slices, fresh spinach leaves, bacon and a sprinkle of blue cheese — this panini will melt in your mouth, leaving you yearning for more.

Serves 2

Variations

If you happen to have a firm, ripe pear, use it in place of the apple.

I also enjoy this sandwich with crumbled feta cheese instead of the blue cheese.

Preheat panini grill to high

2	ciabatta rolls, split	2
1 tbsp	olive oil	15 mL
2 tbsp	honey mustard	25 mL
4 oz	roasted chicken breast, thinly sliced	125 g
½ cup	baby spinach leaves	125 mL
¼ cup	crumbled blue cheese	50 mL
6	thin slices Granny Smith apple (unpeeled)	6
4	slices thick-cut bacon, cooked crisp	4

1. Place rolls, cut side down, on a work surface and brush crusts with oil. Turn rolls over and spread with mustard. On bottom halves, evenly layer with chicken, spinach, blue cheese, apple and bacon. Cover with top halves and press gently to pack.

2. Place sandwiches in grill, close the top plate and cook until golden brown, 3 to 4 minutes. Serve immediately.

Lobster Fontina Panini (page 84)

Grilled Chicken, Spinach, Red Pepper
and Pepper Jack Panini (page 93)

Blue Cheese, Chicken and Apple Panini (page 96)

South of the Border Turkey Panini (page 107)

Turkey Panini with Cranberry Chutney
and Sunflower Seeds (page 110)

Flank Steak, Bacon and Tomato Panini (page 118)

Roast Beef, Boursin, Red Onion and Arugula Panini (page 129)

Sliced Meatball Panini (page 138)

Roasted Chicken, Brie and Pear Panini

Roasted chicken is wonderful with creamy Brie cheese and firm, ripe pears. You can find pears throughout the year. Choose your favorite variety (I like Bosc pears) and enjoy their freshness accented with apricot preserves and red onion.

Serves 2

Tips

Use a sharp paring knife to remove the rind of the Brie.

To store lettuce, wash it under cold running water and dry with paper towels, then wrap it in plastic and place it in the crisper section of your refrigerator.

Preheat panini grill to high

4	slices whole wheat bread (½-inch/1 cm thick slices)	4
1 tbsp	olive oil	15 mL
1 tbsp	mayonnaise	15 mL
1 tbsp	apricot preserves or jam	15 mL
2 oz	roasted chicken breast, thinly sliced	60 g
2 oz	Brie cheese, rind removed, thinly sliced	60 g
2	curly-leaf lettuce leaves	2
2	thin slices red onion	2
1	ripe but firm pear, thinly sliced	1

1. Brush one side of each bread slice with oil. Place on a work surface, oiled side down, and spread mayonnaise over bottom halves. Spread apricot preserves over top halves. On bottom halves, evenly layer with chicken, cheese, lettuce, onion and pear. Cover with top halves and press gently to pack.

2. Place sandwiches in grill, close the top plate and cook until golden brown, 3 to 4 minutes. Serve immediately.

The Meg

These ingredients are my best friend, Meg's, favorite sandwich combination, so we put them in a panini. The Russian dressing adds zest.

Serves 2

Tip

Leaving the apple unpeeled adds to the nutrient value and crunch.

Variation

Substitute French dressing for the Russian dressing.

Preheat panini grill to high

4	slices pumpernickel bread (1-inch/2.5 cm thick slices)	4
1 tbsp	butter, melted	15 mL
2 oz	smoked turkey breast, sliced	60 g
2 oz	Brie cheese, rind removed, thinly sliced	60 g
6	thin slices Granny Smith apple (unpeeled)	6
¼ cup	alfalfa sprouts	50 mL
¼ cup	Russian dressing (store-bought or see recipe, page 235)	50 mL

1. Brush one side of each bread slice with butter. Place on a work surface, buttered side down. On bottom halves, evenly layer with turkey, cheese, apple and sprouts. Drizzle with dressing. Cover with top halves and press gently to pack.

2. Place sandwiches in grill, close the top plate and cook until golden brown, 3 to 4 minutes. Serve immediately.

Turkey in a Jam Panini

You will be amazed by how wonderful this panini tastes, with its surprise ingredient, raspberry jam. I created it by accident, but was truly pleased with the outcome. Come on ... give it a try!

Serves 2

Variations

Add crispy bacon slices for crunch.

Omit the mixed greens and use a few spinach leaves instead.

Preheat panini grill to high

4	slices sourdough bread (½-inch/1 cm thick slices)	4
1 tbsp	butter, melted	15 mL
2 tbsp	raspberry jam	25 mL
2 oz	Swiss cheese, thinly sliced	60 g
2 oz	deli-sliced turkey	60 g
1 cup	mixed greens	250 mL

1. Brush one side of each bread slice with butter. Place on a work surface, buttered side down, and spread with jam. On bottom halves, evenly layer with cheese, turkey and greens. Cover with top halves and press gently to pack.

2. Place sandwiches in grill, close the top plate and cook until golden brown, 3 to 4 minutes. Serve immediately.

Turkey Dijon Panini

The combination of turkey, bacon and cheese makes such a great sandwich, especially when you add fresh tomato and red onion. After a Thanksgiving meal, this is leftover heaven. One year, I failed to purchase sandwich bread and was truly miserable, as the stores are all closed on Thanksgiving evening. I have learned!

Serves 2

Tip

For convenience, have the bakery slice the bread into uniform slices.

Preheat panini grill to high

4	slices French bread (½-inch/1 cm thick slices)	4
1 tbsp	olive oil	15 mL
1 tbsp	Dijon mustard	15 mL
2 oz	Swiss cheese, thinly sliced	60 g
2 oz	roasted turkey breast, thinly sliced	60 g
4	slices thick-cut bacon, cooked crisp	4
4	thin slices tomato	4
4	thin slices red onion	4

1. Brush one side of each bread slice with oil. Place on a work surface, oiled side down, and spread with mustard. On bottom halves, evenly layer with cheese, turkey, bacon, tomato and red onion. Cover with top halves and press gently to pack.

2. Place sandwiches in grill, close the top plate and cook until golden brown, 3 to 4 minutes. Serve immediately.

Honey Dijon Turkey and Cheese Panini

Although the ingredient lineup in this panini is minimal, the flavor is not. Enjoy its simple goodness and remember: it is not quantity but quality that counts.

Serves 2

Variations

If you have deli ham on hand, use it as a substitute for the turkey, or better yet, use both ham and turkey!

Use mayonnaise or a creamy salad dressing in place of the honey Dijon.

Preheat panini grill to high

4	slices sourdough bread (½-inch/1 cm thick slices)	4
1 tbsp	olive oil	15 mL
1 tbsp	honey Dijon mustard	15 mL
4 oz	smoked turkey breast, sliced	125 g
4 oz	provolone cheese, thinly sliced	125 g

1. Brush one side of each bread slice with oil. Place on a work surface, oiled side down, and spread with mustard. On bottom halves, evenly layer with turkey and cheese, alternating layers of each. Cover with top halves and press gently to pack.

2. Place sandwiches in grill, close the top plate and cook until golden brown, 3 to 4 minutes. Serve immediately.

Turkey and Brie Panini with Mushroom Pesto

Mushroom lovers are sure to enjoy this flavor explosion: succulent roasted turkey, Brie, intense mushroom pesto, spinach and sweet onion.

Serves 2

Variations

Spread roasted garlic on the bread for a flavor boost.

Substitute multigrain bread or a unique bread that has been freshly baked at your local bakery or at home, such as pistachio or cranberry loaf.

Preheat panini grill to high

4	slices Italian bread (½-inch/1 cm thick slices)	4
1 tbsp	olive oil	15 mL
⅓ cup	Mushroom Pesto (see recipe, page 246)	75 mL
2 oz	roasted turkey breast, thinly sliced	60 g
2 oz	Brie cheese, rind removed, thinly sliced	60 g
8	large spinach leaves, trimmed	8
2	thin slices sweet onion	2

1. Brush one side of each bread slice with oil. Place two slices on a work surface, oiled side down, and spread with pesto. Evenly layer with turkey, cheese, spinach and onion. Cover with top halves, oiled side up, and press gently to pack.

2. Place sandwiches in grill, close the top plate and cook until golden brown, 3 to 4 minutes. Serve immediately.

Turkey and Bacon Panini

Focaccia makes a hearty foundation for this turkey panini, with Gouda and bacon as flavor accents.

Serves 2

Tip

To save time, purchase prewashed bagged greens and precooked bacon.

Preheat panini grill to high

2	4-inch (10 cm) focaccia, halved horizontally	2
1 tbsp	olive oil	15 mL
2 tbsp	Thousand Island dressing (store-bought or see recipe, page 235)	25 mL
4 oz	smoked turkey breast, thinly sliced	125 g
2 oz	Gouda cheese, thinly sliced	60 g
1 cup	mixed greens	250 mL
4	thin slices tomato	4
4	slices thick-cut bacon, cooked crisp	4

1. Place focaccia, cut side down, on a work surface and brush crusts with oil. Turn focaccia over and brush with dressing. On bottom halves, evenly layer with turkey, cheese, greens, tomato and bacon. Cover with top halves and press gently to pack.

2. Place sandwiches in grill, close the top plate and cook until golden brown, 3 to 4 minutes. Serve immediately.

Spicy Turkey Panini

Chipotle mayonnaise and pepper Jack cheese lend their spiciness to this turkey panini.

Serves 2

Tip

Make sure to drain the sun-dried tomatoes and pat them dry with a paper towel; otherwise, your bread may end up soggy.

Variation

Use flavored tortillas, often found in bakeries or in the bread section of your supermarket, to create spicy turkey quesadillas.

Preheat panini grill to high

2	bolillo rolls (see tip, page 105), split	2
1 tbsp	olive oil	15 mL
2 tbsp	Chipotle Mayonnaise (see recipe, page 237)	25 mL
3 oz	roasted turkey breast, thinly sliced	90 g
2 oz	pepper Jack cheese, sliced	60 g
¼ cup	julienned drained oil-packed sun-dried tomatoes	50 mL
¼ cup	thinly sliced roasted red bell peppers	50 mL

1. Place rolls, cut side down, on a work surface and brush crusts with oil. Turn rolls over and spread with mayonnaise. On bottom halves, evenly layer with turkey, cheese, sun-dried tomatoes and roasted peppers. Cover with top halves and press gently to pack.

2. Place sandwiches in grill, close the top plate and cook until golden brown, 3 to 4 minutes. Serve immediately.

Adobe Panini

This colorful panini features black bean and corn salsa atop roasted turkey and mozzarella cheese. Make extra salsa for dipping, and serve with frozen margaritas.

Serves 2

Tips

Bolillo rolls — one of the most popular breads in Mexico — are made with a basic dough similar to French baguette dough. The rolls have a crispy crust with a soft, chewy crumb. If you can't find them, you can substitute submarine rolls, sourdough rolls or hoagie rolls.

Although I enjoy making flavored mayonnaise, I have found commercial varieties that are very good. A couple of my favorites are chipotle and wasabi mayonnaise.

Variation

Add thinly sliced avocado.

Preheat panini grill to high

2	bolillo rolls, split	2
1 tbsp	olive oil	15 mL
2 tbsp	Chipotle Mayonnaise (see recipe, page 237)	25 mL
3 oz	roasted turkey breast, thinly sliced	90 g
2 oz	mozzarella cheese, sliced	60 g
½ cup	Black Bean and Corn Salsa (see recipe, page 248)	125 mL
¼ cup	sliced green bell pepper	50 mL

1. Place rolls, cut side down, on a work surface and brush crusts with oil. Turn rolls over and spread with mayonnaise. On bottom halves, evenly layer with turkey, cheese, salsa and green pepper. Cover with top halves and press gently to pack.

2. Place sandwiches in grill, close the top plate and cook until golden brown, 3 to 4 minutes. Serve immediately.

Mr. Turkey Pepper Jack Panini

Mr. Turkey Pepper Jack — the name is almost as catchy as the panini is good!

Serves 2

Tip

Red bell peppers, which are the most mature, provide the sweetest flavor.

Variation

Shredded cabbage, especially napa cabbage, would be great substitute for the romaine in this panini. Use ½ cup (125 mL) shredded cabbage.

Preheat panini grill to high

2 tsp	olive oil	10 mL
½	bell pepper (any color), thinly sliced	½
½ cup	thinly sliced white onion	125 mL
Pinch	salt	Pinch
Pinch	freshly ground black pepper	Pinch
4	slices rye bread (½-inch/1 cm thick slices)	4
1 tbsp	butter, melted	15 mL
2 tbsp	mayonnaise	25 mL
2 oz	roasted turkey breast, thinly sliced	60 g
2 oz	pepper Jack cheese, thinly sliced	60 g
2	large romaine lettuce leaves	2

1. In a skillet, heat oil over medium–high heat. Add pepper and onion; sauté until softened and starting to brown, 6 to 9 minutes. Sprinkle with salt and pepper. Remove from heat and keep warm.

2. Brush one side of each bread slice with butter. Place on a work surface, buttered side down, and spread with mayonnaise. On bottom halves, evenly layer with turkey, cheese, lettuce and pepper mixture. Cover with top halves and press gently to pack.

3. Place sandwiches in grill, close the top plate and cook until golden brown, 3 to 4 minutes. Serve immediately.

South of the Border Turkey Panini

Creamy guacamole, Monterey Jack cheese and onion make this a true south of the border treat.

Serves 2

Variations

Add crunch and flavor with crispy bacon strips. The precooked microwavable bacon now found in grocery stores is a real timesaver.

Adding crushed baked tortilla chips to the filling will make this recipe a hit with kids and young adults.

Serve with salsa on the side or add it to the sandwich before pressing.

Preheat panini grill to high

4	slices sourdough bread (½-inch/1 cm thick slices)	4
1 tbsp	butter, melted	15 mL
¼ cup	guacamole (store-bought or see recipe, page 249)	50 mL
2 oz	smoked turkey breast, thinly sliced	60 g
2 oz	Monterey Jack cheese, sliced	60 g
4	thin slices tomato	4
2	romaine lettuce leaves	2
¼ cup	thinly sliced red onion	50 mL

1. Brush one side of each bread slice with butter. Place two slices on a work surface, buttered side down, and spread with guacamole. Evenly layer with turkey, cheese, tomato, lettuce and onion. Cover with top halves, buttered side up, and press gently to pack.

2. Place sandwiches in grill, close the top plate and cook until golden brown, 3 to 4 minutes. Serve immediately.

Strange Turkey Panini

Strange to some, normal to others. I like to put unusual or unexpected ingredients in my recipes — in this case, Gouda, dried cranberries, cucumber, tomato slices and black olives adorn smoked turkey breast.

Serves 2

Variations

For a sweet flavor option, substitute sliced green or red grapes for the cranberries.

Sprinkle with chopped toasted nuts before pressing for added crunch and flavor.

Preheat panini grill to high

2	ciabatta rolls, split	2
1 tbsp	olive oil	15 mL
¼ cup	basil pesto (store-bought or see recipe, page 245)	50 mL
2 oz	smoked turkey breast, thinly sliced	60 g
2 oz	smoked Gouda cheese, thinly sliced	60 g
6	slices cucumber	6
1	small plum (Roma) tomato, thinly sliced	1
¼ cup	dried cranberries	50 mL
¼ cup	sliced drained black olives	50 mL

1. Place rolls, cut side down, on a work surface and brush crusts with oil. Turn rolls over and spread with pesto. On bottom halves, evenly layer with turkey, cheese, cucumber, tomato, cranberries and olives. Cover with top halves and press gently to pack.

2. Place sandwiches in grill, close the top plate and cook until golden brown, 3 to 4 minutes. Serve immediately.

Cranberry Turkey Panini

There is a reason Thanksgiving menus include cranberries, either as sauce, as chutney or in a dessert — it works with turkey, and I love it. You'll be delighted by the combination of roasted turkey (leftovers if you have them), cranberry sauce and cream cheese.

Serves 2

Tip

Cranberry sauce is great in both its whole-berry and jellied forms, but I prefer it whole in this panini.

Preheat panini grill to high

4	slices whole wheat bread (½-inch/1 cm thick slices)	4
1 tbsp	butter, melted	15 mL
¼ cup	cream cheese, softened	50 mL
¼ cup	whole-berry cranberry sauce	50 mL
6 oz	roasted turkey breast, sliced	175 g

1. Brush one side of each bread slice with butter. Place on a work surface, buttered side down, and spread with cream cheese. Spread cranberry sauce over bottom halves, then evenly layer with turkey. Cover with top halves and press gently to pack.

2. Place sandwiches in grill, close the top plate and cook until golden brown, 3 to 4 minutes. Serve immediately.

Turkey Panini with Cranberry Chutney and Sunflower Seeds

I love, love, love this panini. Cranberries and turkey remind me of Thanksgiving, but I don't need to wait for the holiday to enjoy this treat. Sunflower seeds add flavor and a bit of crunch.

Serves 2

Tips

Chutney is a spicy condiment containing fruit, vinegar, sugar and spices from East Indian cuisine. The texture can range from chunky to smooth. If you cannot find cranberry chutney, substitute peach or mango.

I enjoy the flavor of salted sunflower seeds, but unsalted works just as well if you are watching your sodium intake.

Variation

Substitute toasted chopped walnuts for the sunflower seeds.

Preheat panini grill to high

4	slices French bread (½-inch/1 cm thick slices)	4
1 tbsp	olive oil	15 mL
¼ cup	cranberry chutney	50 mL
2 tbsp	mayonnaise	25 mL
3 oz	roasted turkey breast, thinly sliced	90 g
2 oz	Swiss cheese, thinly sliced	60 g
6	thin slices plum (Roma) tomato	6
2	curly-leaf lettuce leaves	2
1 tbsp	roasted salted sunflower seeds	15 mL

1. Brush one side of each bread slice with oil. Place on a work surface, oiled side down, and spread chutney over bottom halves. Spread mayonnaise over top halves. On bottom halves, evenly layer with turkey, cheese, tomato and lettuce. Sprinkle evenly with sunflower seeds. Cover with top halves and press gently to pack.

2. Place sandwiches in grill, close the top plate and cook until golden brown, 3 to 4 minutes. Serve immediately.

Turkey, Avocado and Spinach Panini

Fresh avocado and spinach are enhanced by crisp bacon slices in this turkey panini.

Serves 2

Tip
After slicing the avocado, sprinkle it with citrus juice to keep it from discoloring.

Variation
Bean sprouts or alfalfa sprouts would make a nice addition to this panini.

Preheat panini grill to high

4	slices Italian bread (½-inch/1 cm thick slices)	4
1 tbsp	olive oil	15 mL
2 tbsp	mayonnaise	25 mL
3 oz	roasted turkey breast, thinly sliced	90 g
6	thin slices plum (Roma) tomato	6
4	slices bacon, cooked crisp	4
2	romaine lettuce leaves	2
1	small avocado, thinly sliced	1
½ cup	baby spinach leaves	125 mL
Pinch	salt	Pinch
Pinch	freshly ground black pepper	Pinch

1. Brush one side of each bread slice with oil. Place on a work surface, oiled side down, and spread with mayonnaise. On bottom halves, evenly layer with turkey, tomato, bacon, lettuce, avocado and spinach. Sprinkle with salt and pepper. Cover with top halves and press gently to pack.

2. Place sandwiches in grill, close the top plate and cook until golden brown, 3 to 4 minutes. Serve immediately.

Smoked Turkey, Watercress and Stilton Panini

I used to love these delicate sandwiches. Then I put them in a panini press — and now I am in heaven!

Serves 2

Tip

Did you know that watercress grows in cool running water? This herb is a member of the mustard family and is often found in and around streams and brooks. Watercress has small, crisp, dark green leaves and a pungent, slightly bitter and peppery flavor. Store it, stems down, in a glass of water covered with a plastic bag in the refrigerator for up to 5 days.

Preheat panini grill to high

4	slices whole wheat bread (½-inch/1 cm thick slices)	4
1 tbsp	butter, melted	15 mL
2 tbsp	aïoli (store-bought or see recipe, page 240)	25 mL
2 oz	smoked turkey breast, thinly sliced	60 g
4	thin slices tomato	4
½ cup	watercress, tough stems removed	125 mL
2 oz	Stilton cheese, crumbled	60 g

1. Brush one side of each bread slice with butter. Place two slices on a work surface, buttered side down, and spread with aïoli. Evenly layer with turkey, tomato and watercress. Sprinkle with blue cheese. Cover with top halves, buttered side up, and press gently to pack.

2. Place sandwiches in grill, close the top plate and cook until golden brown, 3 to 4 minutes. Serve immediately.

Turkey and Artichoke Panini

This yummy panini is full of melted goodness!

Serves 2

Tips

If you cannot find focaccia, try sliced sourdough bread instead.

If grated Parmesan is easier, go for it. I just really like the flavor of Parmesan cheese and enjoy the shavings.

Preheat panini grill to high

2	4-inch (10 cm) focaccia, halved horizontally	2
1 tbsp	olive oil	15 mL
2 tbsp	Dijon mustard	25 mL
2 oz	smoked turkey breast, thinly sliced	60 g
2 oz	provolone cheese, thinly sliced	60 g
½ cup	chopped drained artichoke hearts	125 mL
1 tbsp	shaved Parmesan cheese	15 mL

1. Place focaccia, cut side down, on a work surface and brush crusts with oil. Turn focaccia over and spread mustard over bottom halves. Evenly layer with turkey, provolone and artichoke hearts. Sprinkle with Parmesan. Cover with top halves and press gently to pack.

2. Place sandwiches in grill, close the top plate and cook until golden brown, 3 to 4 minutes. Serve immediately.

Mediterranean Gobbler

Rich feta cheese, sun-dried tomatoes and marinated artichoke hearts turn roasted turkey into a Mediterranean dream.

Serves 2

Tip

The best way to melt butter is on the stovetop, as you have more control over the process. However, you can also melt butter in the microwave. Place it in a microwave–safe bowl and microwave on Medium (50%) power for 20 to 40 seconds, checking halfway through and watching for spills.

Preheat panini grill to high

2	4-inch (10 cm) focaccia, halved horizontally	2
1 tbsp	butter, melted	15 mL
2 tbsp	Sun-Dried Tomato Mayonnaise (see recipe, page 236)	25 mL
1/4 cup	crumbled feta cheese	50 mL
3 oz	roasted turkey breast, thinly sliced	90 g
1/4 cup	coarsely chopped drained artichoke hearts	50 mL

1. Place focaccia, cut side down, on a work surface and brush crusts with butter. Turn focaccia over and spread with mayonnaise. Sprinkle feta cheese over bottom halves. Evenly layer with turkey and artichoke hearts. Cover with top halves and press gently to pack.

2. Place sandwiches in grill, close the top plate and cook until golden brown, 3 to 4 minutes. Serve immediately.

Beef Panini

Basil Steak Panini

Fresh basil is so fragrant, so good and so beautiful in this beef panini, which has a bit of an upscale edge but is still great served on a paper plate on your picnic table. Wow, I love the versatility of panini!

Serves 2

Tips

When cooking beef, use an instant–read thermometer to ensure proper doneness. These thermometers are affordable and can often be found at your supermarket.

To lighten up this panini, use part–skim mozzarella cheese.

Preheat panini grill to medium

1	clove garlic, minced	1
¼ tsp	salt	1 mL
¼ tsp	freshly ground lemon pepper	1 mL
2	beef tenderloin steaks (each about 1 inch/2.5 cm thick)	2
2	ciabatta rolls, split	2
1 tbsp	olive oil	15 mL
2 tbsp	Basil Mayonnaise (see recipe, page 236)	25 mL
½ cup	shredded mozzarella cheese	125 mL
¼ cup	fresh basil leaves	50 mL
4	thin slices tomato	4

1. In a bowl, combine garlic, salt and lemon pepper; press evenly into steaks. Arrange steaks on bottom grill plate, close the top plate and grill for 8 to 10 minutes for medium-rare, or to desired doneness. Transfer to a cutting board, cut into thin slices and keep warm. Wipe grill plates clean.

2. Place rolls, cut side down, on a work surface and brush crusts with oil. Turn rolls over and spread with mayonnaise. On bottom halves, evenly layer with steak, cheese, basil and tomato. Cover with top halves and press gently to pack.

3. Place sandwiches in grill, close the top plate and cook until golden brown, 3 to 4 minutes. Serve immediately.

Steak, Bacon and Blue Cheese Panini

Beef tenderloin is my favorite cut of beef, as it is very lean and nutritious. I love a tenderloin steak, wrapped in bacon for added flavor, and cooked to medium-rare on the grill or barbecue, whether on its own, as part of a salad or in a sandwich, as you see here.

Serves 2

Tips

Beef contains a powerhouse of nutrients, including zinc, iron, protein and B vitamins — nutrients that work as hard as you do every day!

I like to cook steaks to medium-rare for maximum flavor and tenderness. A medium-rare steak has an internal temperature of approximately 145°F (63°C).

Preheat panini grill to high

4	slices sourdough bread (½-inch/1 cm thick slices)	4
1 tbsp	olive oil	15 mL
6 oz	beef tenderloin steak, cooked and thinly sliced	175 g
4	slices bacon, cooked crisp	4
⅓ cup	Chipotle Barbecue Sauce (see recipe, page 245)	75 mL
2 tbsp	crumbled blue cheese	25 mL
4	thin slices tomato	4
4	thin slices red onion	4
2	lettuce leaves	2

1. Brush one side of each bread slice with oil. Place two slices on a work surface, oiled side down, and evenly layer with beef and bacon. Drizzle with barbecue sauce and sprinkle with blue cheese. Layer with tomato, red onion and lettuce. Cover with top halves, oiled side up, and press gently to pack.

2. Place sandwiches in grill, close the top plate and cook until golden brown, 3 to 4 minutes. Serve immediately.

Flank Steak, Bacon and Tomato Panini

My favorite salad consists of iceberg lettuce, tomatoes, blue cheese and bacon, dusted with freshly ground black pepper. I added grilled beef and now I have it in a panini — perfect!

Serves 2

Tips

When grilling on the weekend, grill extra meat for weekday panini recipes like this one. Grilled beef makes great leftovers.

Flank steak is a very lean cut of beef that is best prepared using a moist-heat cooking method. However, if you're grilling or broiling it, marinate it in the refrigerator for at least 6 hours to tenderize it.

Preheat panini grill to high

4	slices sourdough bread (½-inch/1 cm thick slices)	4
1 tbsp	olive oil	15 mL
2 tbsp	Blue Cheese Mayonnaise (see recipe, page 237)	25 mL
8 oz	flank steak, grilled and thinly sliced	250 g
½ cup	shredded iceberg lettuce	125 mL
6	slices bacon, cooked crisp	6
4	thin slices tomato	4
Pinch	freshly ground black pepper	Pinch

1. Brush one side of each bread slice with oil. Place on a work surface, oiled side down, and spread with mayonnaise. On bottom halves, evenly layer with steak, lettuce, bacon and tomato. Sprinkle with pepper. Cover with top halves and press gently to pack.

2. Place sandwiches in grill, close the top plate and cook until golden brown, 3 to 4 minutes. Serve immediately.

Roast Beef Panini with Olive Tapenade

I love the versatility of olive tapenade, especially combined with Boursin cheese. I've shared my family recipe for tapenade on page 242, but I have also found numerous commercial brands I enjoy.

Serves 2

Tips

Lighten up this recipe by using light Boursin cheese.

Add unique flavor by choosing a flavored deli roast beef.

Variation

Try this recipe with my favorite bread: sourdough.

Preheat panini grill to high

4	slices Italian bread (1-inch/2.5 cm thick slices)	4
1 tbsp	olive oil	15 mL
2 tbsp	Boursin cheese	25 mL
2 tbsp	good-quality olive tapenade (store-bought or see recipe, page 242)	25 mL
1 tbsp	grainy Dijon (stone-ground) mustard	15 mL
2 oz	roast beef, thinly sliced	60 g
2	red-tipped lettuce leaves	2
½ cup	thinly sliced red onion	125 mL

1. Brush one side of each bread slice with oil. Place on a work surface, oiled side down, and spread cheese and tapenade over bottom halves. Spread mustard over top halves. On bottom halves, evenly layer with beef, lettuce and onion. Cover with top halves and press gently to pack.

2. Place sandwiches in grill, close the top plate and cook until golden, 3 to 4 minutes. Serve immediately.

Beef Panini with Sweet Onion Jam

The flavor of this sweet onion jam, with a hint of vinegar, is perfect with roast beef.

Serves 2

Tip

The sweet onion jam can be stored in an airtight container in the refrigerator for up to 1 week. It tastes great with poultry, pork and vegetables.

Bolillo rolls — one of the most popular breads in Mexico — are made with a basic dough similar to French baguette dough. The rolls have a crispy crust with a soft, chewy crumb. If you can't find them, you can substitute submarine rolls, sourdough rolls or hoagie rolls.

Preheat panini grill to high

Sweet Onion Jam

1 tbsp	canola oil	15 mL
1 cup	thinly sliced red onion	250 mL
1 tbsp	granulated sugar	15 mL
1 tbsp	light (white or golden) corn syrup	15 mL
1 tbsp	cider vinegar	15 mL
Pinch	salt	Pinch
Pinch	freshly ground black pepper	Pinch

Sandwich

2	bolillo rolls, split	2
1 tbsp	olive oil	15 mL
2 oz	roast beef, thinly sliced	60 g
2	lettuce leaves	2

1. *Prepare the jam:* In a skillet, heat oil over medium-high heat. Add onions and sauté until tender, 5 to 7 minutes. Stir in sugar, corn syrup, vinegar, salt and pepper; reduce heat to low and cook, stirring occasionally, until reduced to a thick consistency, 20 to 25 minutes. Remove from heat and keep warm.

2. *Prepare the sandwich:* Place rolls, cut side down, on a work surface and brush crusts with oil. Turn rolls over and, on bottom halves, evenly layer with beef and onion jam. Top with lettuce. Cover with top halves and press gently to pack.

3. Place sandwiches in grill, close the top plate and cook until golden brown, 3 to 4 minutes. Serve immediately.

Beef and Shiitake Panini

There is something wonderful about the combination of beef and mushrooms, especially shiitakes. Baby spinach leaves add both color and nutrients. Serve this recipe with French onion soup for a perfect meal.

Serves 2

Tip

Shiitake mushrooms pair well with beef, but feel free to use your favorite mushroom variety. When cooking with fresh or dried shiitakes, remove and discard the stems, which are fibrous and tough.

Preheat panini grill to high

2 tsp	olive oil	10 mL
4 oz	shiitake mushrooms, stems removed, caps thinly sliced	125 g
1 tbsp	soy sauce	15 mL
1 tsp	Worcestershire sauce	5 mL
4	slices sourdough bread (½-inch1 cm thick slices)	4
1 tbsp	olive oil	15 mL
2 oz	roast beef, thinly sliced	60 g
2 oz	provolone cheese, thinly sliced	60 g
½ cup	baby spinach leaves	125 mL

1. In a skillet, heat oil over medium–high heat. Add mushrooms and sauté until they release their liquid, 3 to 5 minutes. Reduce heat to low and add soy sauce and Worcestershire sauce; cook, stirring occasionally, until liquid is absorbed and mushrooms are tender, 7 to 9 minutes. Remove from heat and keep warm.

2. Brush one side of each bread slice with oil. Place two slices on a work surface, oiled side down, and evenly layer with beef, cheese, spinach and mushroom mixture. Cover with top halves, oiled side up, and press gently to pack.

3. Place sandwiches in grill, close the top plate and cook until golden brown, 3 to 4 minutes. Serve immediately

Horseradish Beef Panini

With this panini, I have tried to replicate the flavor of prime rib cooked rare and served with creamy horseradish sauce.

Serves 2

Variation

For a simple beef panini, substitute sliced sourdough bread for the focaccia, and leave everything off except for the horseradish mayonnaise and beef. But you might as well double the beef!

Preheat panini grill to high

2	4-inch (10 cm) focaccia, halved horizontally	2
1 tbsp	olive oil	15 mL
2 tbsp	Horseradish Mayonnaise (see recipe, page 238)	25 mL
4 oz	roast beef, thinly sliced	125 g
2 oz	smoked Cheddar cheese, sliced	60 g
½ cup	baby spinach leaves	125 mL
¼ cup	thinly sliced red onion	50 mL
4	thin slices tomato	4
2	drained pickled pepperoncini peppers, thinly sliced	2

1. Place focaccia, cut side down, on a work surface and brush crusts with oil. Turn focaccia over and spread with mayonnaise. On bottom halves, evenly layer with beef, cheese, spinach, onion, tomato and peppers. Cover with top halves and press gently to pack.

2. Place sandwiches in grill, close the top plate and cook until golden brown, 3 to 4 minutes. Serve immediately.

Beef with a Kick Panini

As a native Texan, I love beef and I love spicy foods, which is why I paired beef with jalapeño peppers. The creamy pepper Jack cheese gives this panini an additional kick without overpowering it.

Serves 2

Tip

Peppered roast beef from the deli counter would be particularly wonderful in this panini, but make sure to adjust the other spicy ingredients to your taste.

Preheat panini grill to high

2	ciabatta rolls, split	2
1 tbsp	butter, melted	15 mL
1 tbsp	mayonnaise	15 mL
2 oz	roast beef, thinly sliced	60 g
2 oz	pepper Jack cheese, thinly sliced	60 g
¼ cup	drained sliced pickled jalapeño peppers	50 mL
¼ cup	chopped onion	50 mL

1. Place rolls, cut side down, on a work surface and brush crusts with butter. Turn rolls over and spread with mayonnaise. On bottom halves, evenly layer with beef, cheese, jalapeños and onion. Cover with top halves and press gently to pack.

2. Place sandwiches in grill, close the top plate and cook until golden brown, 3 to 4 minutes. Serve immediately.

Chipotle Beef Panini

Chipotle peppers are dried, smoked jalapeños. Combined with mayonnaise, they add a spicy, smoky flavor accent to this beef panini.

Serves 2

Tip

Swiss-style cheeses are good for sandwiches and salads and have excellent melting properties. Baby Swiss cheese has smaller holes and a milder flavor than regular Swiss cheese. Either will work beautifully in this recipe.

Variation

For a spicier panini, use jalapeño Jack cheese instead of Swiss and add diced jalapeños.

Preheat panini grill to high

4	slices French bread (½-inch/1 cm thick slices)	4
1 tbsp	butter, melted	15 mL
2 tbsp	Chipotle Mayonnaise (see recipe, page 237)	25 mL
2 oz	roast beef, thinly sliced	60 g
2 oz	baby Swiss cheese, thinly sliced	60 g
6	thin slices plum (Roma) tomato	6
4	thin slices sweet onion	4

1. Brush one side of each bread slice with butter. Place on a work surface, buttered side down, and spread with mayonnaise. On bottom halves, evenly layer with beef, cheese, tomato and onion. Cover with top halves and press gently to pack.

2. Place sandwiches in grill, close the top plate and cook until golden brown, 3 to 4 minutes. Serve immediately

Spicy Roast Beef and Avocado Panini

Chipotle mayonnaise, beef, Monterey Jack cheese, hot pepper sauce and avocado are a perfect flavor combination. Make sure to use perfectly ripened avocados.

Serves 2

Tips

Picking the perfect avocado is hard to do, as they go so quickly from perfectly ripe to way too ripe. It's best to choose slightly unripe ones and let them ripen on the counter, much as you would with bananas. Purchase avocados that are dark green, heavy for their size and hard (if you are going to use them right away, they should yield to gentle thumb pressure).

If you prefer, mash the avocado and use it as a spread.

Preheat panini grill to high

2	bolillo rolls (see tip, page 120), split	2
1 tbsp	olive oil	15 mL
2 tbsp	Chipotle Mayonnaise (see recipe, page 237)	25 mL
3 oz	roast beef, thinly sliced	90 g
2 oz	Monterey Jack cheese, sliced	60 g
1	small avocado, thinly sliced	1
½ tsp	hot pepper sauce (or to taste)	2 mL

1. Place rolls, cut side down, on a work surface and brush crusts with oil. Turn rolls over and spread with mayonnaise. On bottom halves, evenly layer with beef, cheese and avocado. Sprinkle with hot pepper sauce. Cover with top halves and press gently to pack.

2. Place sandwiches in grill, close the top plate and cook until golden brown, 3 to 4 minutes. Serve immediately.

Cheesy Beef Panini

This wonderfully overstuffed panini has a melting of Cheddar and mozzarella cheeses. I have had rave reviews of this sandwich and love making it for friends and family.

Serves 2

Tip

Be careful when placing this sandwich in the panini maker. Make sure to gently lower the top plate to ensure that the filling does not ooze out. I keep a wooden spoon or spatula handy to assist in keeping ingredients inside during the pressing process. If you have a panini maker with a floating top plate, this works very well.

Preheat panini grill to high

1 tbsp	olive oil	15 mL
½ cup	sliced mushrooms	125 mL
½ cup	sliced green bell pepper	125 mL
¼ cup	sliced sweet onion	50 mL
4	slices sourdough bread (½-inch/1 cm thick slices)	4
1 tbsp	butter, melted	15 mL
2 tbsp	Horseradish Mayonnaise (see recipe, page 238)	25 mL
2 oz	roast beef, sliced	60 g
1 oz	Cheddar cheese, thinly sliced	30 g
1 oz	mozzarella cheese, thinly sliced	30 g

1. In a large nonstick skillet, heat oil over medium heat. Add mushrooms, green pepper and onion; sauté until tender, 7 to 9 minutes. Remove from heat and keep warm.

2. Brush one side of each bread slice with butter. Place on a work surface, buttered side down, and spread with mayonnaise. On bottom halves, evenly layer with beef, Cheddar, mozzarella and mushroom mixture. Cover with top halves and press gently to pack.

3. Place sandwiches in grill, close the top plate so that it barely touches the sandwiches and cook until golden brown, 3 to 4 minutes. Serve immediately.

Beef and Brie Panini

I adore this recipe, which combines lean roast beef with beautifully melted Brie, my favorite cheese. The combination of horseradish mayonnaise and Dijon mustard is wonderful. I am really not sure that it gets any better than this.

Serves 2

Tip

In my local supermarket, I have found deli roast beef cooked rare! What an amazing treat, especially for this recipe.

Preheat panini grill to high

1	clove garlic, minced	1
2 tbsp	butter, softened	25 mL
1 tsp	chopped fresh oregano	5 mL
1 tsp	chopped fresh parsley	5 mL
4	slices sourdough bread (½-inch/1 cm thick slices)	4
1 tbsp	Horseradish Mayonnaise (see recipe, page 238)	15 mL
1 tbsp	Dijon mustard	15 mL
2 oz	roast beef, thinly sliced	60 g
2 oz	Brie cheese, rind removed, thinly sliced	60 g

1. In a bowl, combine garlic, butter, oregano and parsley.

2. Spread one side of each bread slice with the butter mixture. Place on a work surface, buttered side down, and spread mayonnaise over bottom halves. Spread mustard over top halves. On bottom halves, evenly layer with beef and cheese. Cover with top halves and press gently to pack.

3. Place sandwiches in grill, close the top plate and cook until golden brown, 3 to 4 minutes. Serve immediately.

Roast Beef, Cheddar and Red Onion Panini

Grilled onions are a terrific accent for beef. During the grilling process, the natural sugars in the onions caramelize, producing amazing flavor. In this recipe, I use my panini grill to cook the onions. When using my outdoor grill or barbecue, I grill several onions at once to use throughout the week.

Serves 2

Tips

Commercial horseradish spreads are a good alternative to homemade, though you have to trade off freshness for convenience.

Ciabatta rolls are a great foundation for most panini recipes, and especially this one, but variety is the key, so use whatever bread suits your fancy in the moment.

Preheat panini grill to high

½	small red onion, cut into thin slices	½
2 tbsp	olive oil, divided	25 mL
Pinch	salt	Pinch
Pinch	freshly ground black pepper	Pinch
2	ciabatta rolls, split	2
2 tbsp	Creamy Horseradish Sauce (see recipe, page 243)	25 mL
2 oz	roast beef, thinly sliced	60 g
2 oz	Cheddar cheese, sliced	60 g

1. Brush onion slices with 2 tsp (10 mL) of the oil. Sprinkle with salt and pepper. Arrange on bottom grill plate, close the top plate and grill until tender and lightly charred, 2 to 3 minutes. Transfer to a plate and keep warm. Wipe grill plates clean.

2. Place rolls, cut side down, on a work surface and brush crusts with the remaining oil. Turn rolls over and spread with horseradish sauce. On bottom halves, evenly layer with beef, cheese and grilled onions. Cover with top halves and press gently to pack.

3. Place sandwiches in grill, close the top plate and cook until golden brown, 3 to 4 minutes. Serve immediately.

Roast Beef, Boursin, Red Onion and Arugula Panini

Versatile Boursin cheese works so well with beef, red onion and arugula, creating a melted burst of flavor that is sure to satisfy.

Serves 2

Tips

Imported from France, Boursin — perhaps the best known of the triple-cream cheeses — is a rich, soft, uncured cheese that is often infused with herbs, garlic or cracked pepper. It has a delicate flavor and a velvety consistency. I use this amazing cheese in many recipes and serve it on a cheese board for elegant entertaining.

Serve with fresh grapes and strawberries to complement the flavors.

Preheat panini grill to high

2	bolillo rolls (see tip, page 120), split	2
1 tbsp	olive oil	15 mL
3 tbsp	Boursin cheese	45 mL
2 oz	roast beef, thinly sliced	60 g
½ cup	arugula, stemmed	125 mL
¼ cup	sliced red onion	50 mL

1. Place rolls, cut side down, on a work surface and brush crusts with oil. Turn rolls over and spread with cheese. On bottom halves, evenly layer with beef, arugula and onion. Cover with top halves and press gently to pack.

2. Place sandwiches in grill, close the top plate and cook until golden brown, 3 to 4 minutes. Serve immediately.

Beef, Caramelized Onions and Blue Cheese Panini

The sweetness of caramelized onions and the bite of blue cheese kick this beef panini up a notch.

Serves 2

Tip

At the deli counter in your supermarket, you will find numerous flavors of roast beef, such as peppered and garlic-favored. When using a flavored roast beef, review your ingredient lineup to make sure you don't overpower the panini with too many contrasting flavors.

Preheat panini grill to high

4	slices sourdough bread (1-inch/2.5 cm thick slices)	4
1 tbsp	olive oil	15 mL
2 oz	roast beef, thinly sliced	60 g
½ cup	Caramelized Onions (see recipe, page 248)	125 mL
¼ cup	crumbled blue cheese	50 mL

1. Brush one side of each bread slice with oil. Place two slices on a work surface, oiled side down. Evenly layer with beef, caramelized onions and blue cheese. Cover with top halves, oiled side up, and press gently to pack.

2. Place sandwiches in grill, close the top plate and cook until golden brown, 3 to 4 minutes. Serve immediately.

Feta Beef Panini

Roasted red peppers, feta cheese and tahini dressing add Greek flair to this panini. I used focaccia, as I love its density, but other types of flatbread or pita bread would work well too.

Serves 2

Tip

Deli roast beef is low in fat and calories, but gives me tons of energy for workouts.

Preheat panini grill to high

2	4-inch (10 cm) focaccia, halved horizontally	2
1 tbsp	olive oil	15 mL
2 oz	roast beef, thinly sliced	60 g
1/3 cup	thinly sliced roasted red bell pepper	75 mL
1/2 cup	baby spinach leaves	125 mL
1/4 cup	crumbled feta cheese	50 mL
1/4 cup	Tahini Dressing (see recipe, page 234)	50 mL
Pinch	freshly ground black pepper	Pinch

1. Place focaccia, cut side down, on a work surface and brush crusts with oil. Turn focaccia over and, on bottom halves, evenly layer with beef, roasted pepper and spinach. Sprinkle with feta and drizzle with dressing. Sprinkle with pepper. Cover with top halves and press gently to pack.

2. Place sandwiches in grill, close the top plate and cook until golden brown, 3 to 4 minutes. Serve immediately.

Beef Pizza Panini

It never fails: anytime I include pizza ingredients in a recipe, it is a savory success.

Serves 2

Tip

If you don't like olives, just leave them off.

Preheat panini grill to high

2	Italian rolls, split	2
1 tbsp	olive oil	15 mL
⅔ cup	marinara or pizza sauce	150 mL
2 oz	roast beef, thinly sliced	60 g
½ cup	shredded mozzarella cheese	125 mL
¼ cup	sliced drained black olives	50 mL
¼ cup	sliced drained green olives	50 mL
2 tsp	dried basil	10 mL

1. Place rolls, cut side down, on a work surface and brush crusts with oil. Turn rolls over and spread with marinara sauce. On bottom halves, evenly layer with beef, cheese and black and green olives. Sprinkle with basil. Cover with top halves and press gently to pack.

2. Place sandwiches in grill, close the top plate and cook until golden brown, 3 to 4 minutes. Serve immediately.

Corned Beef and Fontina Panini

Corned beef, spicy mustard and tart dill pickle slices give this panini a sassy attitude. I had to tone it down a bit by adding fontina cheese.

Serves 2

Tips

Serve with creamy coleslaw or potato salad.

If you can find it, marbled rye bread makes a flavorful and beautiful panini.

Preheat panini grill to high

4	slices pumpernickel bread (½-inch/1 cm thick slices)	4
1 tbsp	butter, melted	15 mL
2 tbsp	spicy mustard	25 mL
4 oz	corned beef, thinly sliced	125 g
2 oz	fontina cheese, thinly sliced	60 g
6	slices dill pickle	6
4	thin slices onion	4

1. Brush one side of each bread slice with butter. Place on a work surface, buttered side down, and spread with mustard. On bottom halves, evenly layer with beef, cheese, pickle and onion. Cover with top halves and press gently to pack.

2. Place sandwiches in grill, close the top plate and cook until golden brown, 3 to 4 minutes. Serve immediately.

Bronx Panini

Numerous delicatessens in the New York area make a version of this sandwich. I turned it into a panini even my Yankee friends love.

Serves 2

Tips

Thousand Island dressing is simple to make, but in a pinch you can use store-bought dressing. I prefer the brands that are displayed cold in the produce section.

For a richer flavor, toast the caraway seeds in the microwave or in a nonstick skillet.

Preheat panini grill to high

4	slices pumpernickel bread (1-inch/2.5 cm thick slices)	4
1 tbsp	butter, melted	15 mL
2 tbsp	Thousand Island dressing (store-bought or see recipe, page 235)	25 mL
4 oz	corned beef, thinly sliced	125 g
2 oz	Swiss cheese, sliced	60 g
1 cup	well-drained coleslaw	250 mL
Pinch	caraway seeds	Pinch

1. Brush one side of each bread slice with butter. Place two slices on a work surface, buttered side down, and spread with dressing. Evenly layer with beef, cheese and coleslaw. Sprinkle with caraway seeds. Cover with top halves, buttered side up, and press gently to pack.

2. Place sandwiches in grill, close the top plate and cook until golden brown, 3 to 4 minutes. Serve immediately.

Classic Reuben Panini

The classic Reuben sandwich is a popular hit, and works well as a panini.

Serves 2

Tips

Traditionally, a Reuben sandwich is made with corned beef, Swiss cheese, sauerkraut and Russian dressing on rye bread, but I've seen it made with different types of bread and dressing, and without sauerkraut or Swiss cheese. You can decide for yourself what your definition of a Reuben sandwich is.

Variation

For a Rachel sandwich, substitute pastrami for the corned beef, Thousand Island dressing for the Russian and coleslaw for the sauerkraut.

Preheat panini grill to high

4	slices marbled rye bread (1-inch/2.5 cm thick slices)	4
1 tbsp	butter, melted	15 mL
2 tbsp	Russian dressing (store-bought or see recipe, page 235)	25 mL
2 oz	corned beef, thinly sliced	60 g
2 oz	Swiss cheese, sliced	60 g
⅓ cup	well-drained sauerkraut	75 mL

1. Brush one side of each bread slice with butter. Place two slices on a work surface, buttered side down, and spread with dressing. Evenly layer with beef, cheese and sauerkraut. Cover with top halves, buttered side up, and press gently to pack.

2. Place sandwiches in grill, close the top plate and cook until golden brown, 3 to 4 minutes. Serve immediately.

Pastrami Reuben Panini

This sandwich is much like the Classic Reuben (page 135), but I changed the bread and dressing, added stone-ground mustard and used pastrami instead of corned beef. You can compare the two and see which you like better.

Serves 2

Tip

Serve with crisp kettle potato chips, dill pickles and an ice-cold drink.

Preheat panini grill to high

4	slices rye bread (½-inch/1 cm thick slices)	4
1 tbsp	butter, melted	15 mL
2 tsp	Thousand Island dressing (store-bought or see recipe, page 235)	10 mL
2 tsp	grainy Dijon (stone-ground) mustard	10 mL
2 oz	pastrami, sliced	60 g
2 oz	Swiss cheese, thinly sliced	60 g
⅓ cup	well-drained sauerkraut	75 mL

1. Brush one side of each bread slice with butter. Place on a work surface, buttered side down, and spread dressing over bottom halves. Spread mustard over top halves. On bottom halves, evenly layer with pastrami, cheese and sauerkraut. Cover with top halves and press gently to pack.

2. Place sandwiches in grill, close the top plate and cook until golden brown, 3 to 4 minutes. Serve immediately.

Two-Beef Panini

Corned beef and pastrami have very different flavors, but both are equally good. Why choose between them when you can have both?

Serves 2

Tip
I like to serve this panini with a smear of light mayo and dill pickles.

Preheat panini grill to high

4	slices sourdough bread (½-inch/1 cm thick slices)	4
1 tbsp	butter, melted	15 mL
2 tbsp	honey mustard	25 mL
3 oz	provolone cheese, thinly sliced	90 g
2 oz	corned beef, thinly sliced	60 g
2 oz	pastrami, thinly sliced	60 g
2	lettuce leaves	2
2	plum (Roma) tomatoes, thinly sliced	2

1. Brush one side of each bread slice with butter. Place on a work surface, buttered side down, and spread with mustard. On bottom halves, evenly layer with half the cheese, then with corned beef, pastrami, the remaining cheese, lettuce and tomatoes. Cover with top halves and press gently to pack.

2. Place sandwiches in grill, close the top plate and cook until golden brown, 3 to 4 minutes. Serve immediately.

Sliced Meatball Panini

Meatball subs are delicious, but they can be tricky to eat without making a mess. So I sliced the meatballs to create an even sandwich and make things easier. The mix of two perfect melting cheeses, mozzarella and provolone, adds wonderful flavor to this recipe.

Serves 2

Tips

Fully cooked meatballs can be found in the frozen food section of most supermarkets, or you can use your own recipe.

I like to cut the basil into chiffonade: stack the basil leaves, then roll them up tightly. Thinly slice across the rolled leaves with a sharp knife to produce fine ribbons.

Preheat panini grill to high

2 tbsp	olive oil, divided	25 mL
8	cooked meatballs (about 1 inch/2.5 cm), cut into 3 or 4 slices	8
1 cup	marinara sauce	250 mL
2	hoagie buns, split	2
2 oz	provolone cheese, thinly sliced	60 g
¼ cup	thinly sliced fresh basil	50 mL
¼ cup	shredded mozzarella cheese	50 mL
2 tbsp	freshly grated Parmesan cheese	25 mL

1. In a skillet, heat 2 tsp (10 mL) of the oil over medium heat. Add sliced meatballs and cook, turning once, until browned on both sides, 4 to 5 minutes. Add marinara sauce, reduce heat to low and simmer until meatballs are heated through, 8 to 10 minutes. Remove from heat and keep warm.

2. Place buns, cut side down, on a work surface and brush crusts with the remaining oil. Turn rolls over and, on bottom halves, evenly layer with provolone, meatballs and sauce. Sprinkle with basil, mozzarella and Parmesan. Cover with top halves and press gently to pack.

3. Place sandwiches in grill, close the top plate so that it barely touches the sandwiches and cook until golden brown, 3 to 4 minutes. Serve immediately.

Pork Panini

The Cuban

You will find numerous variations of the Cuban sandwich, but this one, with succulent pork, spicy mustard, delicate cheese and, of course, a dill pickle, is my favorite.

Serves 2

Tips

Gruyère cheese has a rich, sweet, nutty flavor that is highly prized both for out-of-hand eating and cooking.

A Cuban sandwich typically offers a plethora of ingredients, including pork, cheese, pickles, mustard and Cuban bread. This sandwich originated in Cuba and was brought to the U.S. via the southern Florida communities of Miami and Tampa.

Preheat panini grill to high

2	6-inch (15 cm) French baguettes or hoagie rolls, split	2
1 tbsp	olive oil	15 mL
1 tbsp	spicy mustard	15 mL
2 oz	deli roast pork, thinly sliced	60 g
2 oz	smoked ham, thinly sliced	60 g
2 oz	Gruyère or Swiss cheese, thinly sliced	60 g
1	large dill pickle, thinly sliced lengthwise	1

1. Place baguettes, cut side down, on a work surface and brush crusts with oil. Turn baguettes over and spread with mustard. On bottom halves, evenly layer with pork, ham, cheese and pickle slices. Cover with top halves and press gently to pack.

2. Place sandwiches in grill, close the top plate and cook until golden brown, 3 to 4 minutes. Serve immediately.

Fontina and Capicola Panini

Although capicola is a bit more expensive than most salami, it is worth the price in this recipe, where it's paired with fontina and arugula.

Serves 2

Tips

Capicola is an Italian cold cut made from dry-cured pork shoulder. In addition to its use as a sandwich filling, it also makes a wonderful antipasto or pizza topping.

Fontina has a mild, nutty flavor and melts easily and smoothly, which makes it perfect for panini.

Preheat panini grill to high

2	ciabatta rolls, split	2
1 tbsp	olive oil	15 mL
2 oz	capicola, thinly sliced	60 g
2 oz	fontina cheese, thinly sliced	60 g
½ cup	arugula	125 mL

1. Place rolls, cut side down, on a work surface and brush crusts with oil. Turn rolls over and, on bottom halves, evenly layer with capicola, cheese and arugula. Cover with top halves and press gently to pack

2. Place sandwiches in grill, close the top plate and cook until golden brown, 3 to 4 minutes. Serve immediately.

Ham and Swiss Panini

Ham and Swiss cheese sandwiches are great as is, but wait until you taste one warm from your panini grill. Adding bacon to the mix enlivens the flavor.

Serves 2

Tip

Mustard seeds have been used for culinary purposes since prehistoric times. You will find mention of them in the Bible.

Variation

Substitute hearty wheat or white bread for the rye.

Preheat panini grill to high

4	slices rye bread (1/2-inch/1 cm thick slices)	4
1 tbsp	butter, melted	15 mL
1 tbsp	Dijon mustard	15 mL
2 oz	Swiss cheese, thinly sliced	60 g
2 oz	smoked ham, thinly sliced	60 g
4	slices thick-cut bacon, cooked crisp	4
4	thin slices tomato	4
Pinch	salt	Pinch
Pinch	freshly ground black pepper	Pinch

1. Brush one side of each bread slice with butter. Place on a work surface, buttered side down, and spread with mustard. On bottom halves, evenly layer with cheese, ham, bacon and tomato. Sprinkle with salt and pepper. Cover with top halves and press gently to pack.

2. Place sandwiches in grill, close the top plate and cook until golden brown, 3 to 4 minutes. Serve immediately.

Monte Cristo Panini

A classic Monte Cristo consists of Gruyère cheese and lean ham between two slices of bread, dipped in egg and fried in clarified butter. It was originally served in 1910 in a Paris café. I have taken this famous sandwich and put my own spin on it, creating wonderful flavor with a hint of cinnamon.

Serves 2

Tips

Leave out the cinnamon if you are not a fan. This sandwich is wonderful sprinkled with icing sugar alone!

I love eating this like French toast, with a side of hot maple syrup.

Variation

Add a slice of turkey to each sandwich for a meatier Monte Cristo.

Preheat panini grill to high

4	slices French bread (½-inch/1 cm thick slices)	4
1 tbsp	butter, melted	15 mL
1 tbsp	yellow mustard	15 mL
2 oz	Swiss cheese, thinly sliced	60 g
2 oz	smoked ham, thinly sliced	60 g
1	egg	1
1 tbsp	milk	15 mL
1 tsp	confectioner's (icing) sugar	5 mL
¼ tsp	ground cinnamon	1 mL

1. Brush one side of each bread slice with butter. Place on a work surface, buttered side down, and spread with mustard. On bottom halves, evenly layer with cheese and ham. Cover with top halves and press gently to pack.

2. In a pie plate, whisk together egg and milk. Dip both sides of each sandwich in egg mixture.

3. In a small bowl, combine sugar and cinnamon; set aside.

4. Place sandwiches in grill, close the top plate and cook until golden brown, 3 to 4 minutes. Sift sugar mixture over each panini. Serve immediately.

Ham and Gouda Panini

An easy ingredient list gives you a perfect blend of flavor. Smoked Gouda pairs well with honey mustard.

Serves 2

Tips

Honey mustard is most often used as a spread for sandwiches and as a dip for french fries, onion rings and other finger foods.

I like the density of bolillo rolls for this panini, but any bread variety will work well.

Preheat panini grill to high

2	bolillo rolls (see tip, page 120), split	2
1 tbsp	olive oil	15 mL
1 tbsp	honey mustard	15 mL
3 oz	baked ham, thinly sliced	90 g
2 oz	smoked Gouda cheese, thinly sliced	60 g

1. Place rolls, cut side down, on a work surface and brush crusts with oil. Turn rolls over and spread with mustard. On bottom halves, evenly layer with ham and cheese. Cover with top halves and press gently to pack.

2. Place sandwiches in grill, close the top plate and cook until golden brown, 3 to 4 minutes. Serve immediately.

Ham, Smoked Mozzarella and Tomato Panini

For the best combination of flavors, serve this succulent panini with a crisp white wine.

Serves 2

Tips

If you cannot find smoked mozzarella, try creamy buffalo mozzarella or use your favorite variety.

For an easy but delicious snack or appetizer, toast bread in your panini grill, top with mozzarella and sprinkle with salt, pepper and a little olive oil.

Preheat panini grill to high

2	ciabatta rolls, split	2
1 tbsp	olive oil	15 mL
2 tbsp	mayonnaise	25 mL
4 oz	baked ham, thinly sliced	125 g
2 oz	smoked mozzarella cheese, sliced	60 g
4	thin slices tomato	4

1. Place rolls, cut side down, on a work surface and brush crusts with oil. Turn rolls over and spread with mayonnaise. On bottom halves, evenly layer with ham, cheese and tomato. Cover with top halves and press gently to pack.

2. Place sandwiches in grill, close the top plate and cook until golden brown, 3 to 4 minutes. Serve immediately

Grilled Ham, Brie and Blue Cheese Panini with Peach Preserves

Delicate Brie and tangy blue cheese balance the sweetness of peach preserves in this panini.

Serves 2

Tip

Blue cheese is believed to have been originally created by accident. The caves that early cheeses were aged in, while they were temperature- and moisture-controlled environments, were also favorable to many varieties of mold.

Preheat panini grill to high

4	slices hearty wheat bread (1-inch/2.5 cm thick slices)	4
1 tbsp	butter, melted	15 mL
¼ cup	peach preserves or jam	50 mL
3 oz	Black Forest ham, thinly sliced	90 g
2 oz	Brie cheese, rind removed, thinly sliced	60 g
2 tbsp	crumbled blue cheese	25 mL

1. Brush one side of each bread slice with butter. Place on a work surface, buttered side down, and spread with peach preserves. On bottom halves, evenly layer with ham, Brie and blue cheese. Cover with top halves and press gently to pack.

2. Place sandwiches in grill, close the top plate and cook until golden brown, 3 to 4 minutes. Serve immediately.

Cheddar, Ham and Apple Panini

The sweet and spicy flavor of mango chutney adds a bit of flair to ham, Cheddar and apple.

**Serves 2
as an appetizer**

Tip

Chutney is a spicy and sweet condiment containing fruit, vinegar, sugar and spices. Chutneys range from chunky to smooth in texture and from mild to hot in spiciness.

Preheat panini grill to high

2	ciabatta rolls, split	2
1 tbsp	butter, melted	15 mL
¼ cup	mango chutney	50 mL
2 oz	baked ham, thinly sliced	60 g
2 oz	Cheddar cheese, thinly sliced	60 g
½	Granny Smith apple, thinly sliced	½

1. Place rolls, cut side down, on a work surface and brush crusts with butter. Turn rolls over and spread with chutney. On bottom halves, evenly layer with ham, cheese and apple. Cover with top halves and press gently to pack.

2. Place sandwiches in grill, close the top plate and cook until golden brown, 3 to 4 minutes. Serve immediately.

Prosciutto, Melon and Brie Panini

Prosciutto is perfect with melon, either honeydew or cantaloupe. Brie secures the ingredients and provides a rich flavor.

**Serves 2
as an appetizer**

Tips

Be careful not to overpower this delicate panini with a strongly flavored focaccia, such as those flavored with rosemary, olives or sun-dried tomatoes.

Mesclun mix makes a great addition to this recipe.

Preheat panini grill to high

2	4-inch (10 cm) focaccia, halved horizontally	2
1 tbsp	olive oil	15 mL
2 tbsp	balsamic vinegar	25 mL
2 oz	Brie cheese, rind removed, thinly sliced	60 g
2 oz	prosciutto, thinly sliced	60 g
4	thin slices honeydew or cantaloupe melon	4

1. Place focaccia, cut side down, on a work surface and brush crusts with oil. Turn focaccia over and brush with vinegar. On bottom halves, evenly layer with cheese, prosciutto and melon. Cover with top halves and press gently to pack.

2. Place sandwiches in grill, close the top plate and cook until golden brown, 3 to 4 minutes. Serve immediately.

Cheesy Prosciutto Panini

This upscale recipe features classic prosciutto and a duo of cheeses.

Serves 2

Tip

Prosciutto is an aged, dry-cured, spiced Italian ham that is usually sold in super-thin slices. It's best eaten as is, as a first course with figs or melon slices. Prolonged cooking toughens it.

Preheat panini grill to high

4	slices sourdough bread (½-inch/1 cm thick slices)	4
1 tbsp	olive oil	15 mL
2 oz	prosciutto di Parma, thinly sliced	60 g
2 oz	Gouda cheese, thinly sliced	60 g
2 oz	mozzarella cheese, thinly sliced	60 g

1. Brush one side of each bread slice with oil. Place two slices on a work surface, oiled side down, and evenly layer with prosciutto, Gouda and mozzarella. Cover with top halves, oiled side up, and press gently to pack.

2. Place sandwiches in grill, close the top plate and cook until golden brown, 3 to 4 minutes. Serve immediately.

Prosciutto and Smoked Gouda Panini

Brushing the bread with a mixture of balsamic vinegar and olive oil gives it a fragrance and unique flavor that melds perfectly with the smoked Gouda and prosciutto.

Serves 2 as an appetizer

Tip

Grades of balsamic vinegar vary; therefore, their uses should vary. Young vinegars of 3 to 5 years are used in salad dressings, while vinegars of 6 to 12 years are used to enhance sauces, pastas and risottos. Rich, thick vinegars of more than 12 years are used sparsely to enhance plain meat or fish. I love a drizzle of aged balsamic vinegar over fresh, ripe strawberries.

Preheat panini grill to high

2 tbsp	olive oil	25 mL
1 tbsp	balsamic vinegar	15 mL
4	slices Italian bread (½-inch/1 cm thick slices)	4
2 oz	smoked Gouda cheese, thinly sliced	60 g
2 oz	prosciutto, thinly sliced	60 g
4	thin slices tomato	4
Pinch	salt	Pinch
Pinch	freshly ground black pepper	Pinch

1. In a bowl, whisk together oil and vinegar.

2. Brush one side of each bread slice with the oil mixture. Place two slices on a work surface, oiled side down, and evenly layer with cheese, prosciutto and tomato. Sprinkle with salt and pepper. Cover with top halves, oiled side up, and press gently to pack.

3. Place sandwiches in grill, close the top plate and cook until golden brown, 3 to 4 minutes. Serve immediately.

Prosciutto, Asparagus and Provolone Panini

Delicate prosciutto and asparagus make a beautiful sandwich, perfect for entertaining.

Serves 2

Tips

Be careful when cooking the asparagus: overcooking it will give you soft spears that just do not have the texture needed for this recipe.

For the perfect lunch, serve with crisp bagel chips and bottled sparkling water with a splash of fresh orange juice.

Preheat panini grill to high

8	spears asparagus	8
4	slices pumpernickel bread (1-inch/2.5 cm thick slices)	4
1 tbsp	butter, melted	15 mL
2 tbsp	Basil Mayonnaise (see recipe, page 236)	25 mL
2 oz	prosciutto, thinly sliced	60 g
2 oz	provolone cheese, thinly sliced	60 g
4	thin slices tomato	4
Pinch	salt	Pinch
Pinch	freshly ground black pepper	Pinch

1. Snap off tough ends of asparagus. In a pot of boiling water, cook asparagus until tender–crisp, about 3 minutes. Drain and plunge into ice water to stop the cooking process; drain again and set aside.

2. Brush one side of each bread slice with butter. Place on a work surface, buttered side down, and spread with mayonnaise. On bottom halves, evenly layer with asparagus, prosciutto, cheese and tomato. Sprinkle with salt and pepper. Cover with top halves and press gently to pack.

3. Place sandwiches in grill, close the top plate and cook until golden brown, 3 to 4 minutes. Serve immediately.

Prosciutto, Mozzarella, Basil and Tomato Panini

I love growing basil, and it thrives in my home state of Texas. There is nothing more rewarding than harvesting fresh basil from my small garden to use in my recipes.

Serves 2

Tips

When growing basil, pinch off the flowers and trim the tops to create a bushy plant; otherwise, it will get leggy.

As a snack, I love fresh tomatoes with salt and pepper and a splash of good-quality balsamic vinegar. I use kosher salt, as it seems to melt when it hits the surface of the tomatoes.

Preheat panini grill to high

2	4-inch (10 cm) focaccia, halved horizontally	2
1 tbsp	olive oil	15 mL
2 oz	mozzarella cheese, thinly sliced	60 g
2 oz	prosciutto, thinly sliced	60 g
8	basil leaves	8
6	thin slices tomato	6
Pinch	salt	Pinch
Pinch	freshly ground black pepper	Pinch

1. Place focaccia, cut side down, on a work surface and brush crusts with oil. Turn focaccia over and, on bottom halves, evenly layer with cheese, prosciutto, basil and tomato. Sprinkle with salt and pepper. Cover with top halves and press gently to pack.

2. Place sandwiches in grill, close the top plate and cook until golden brown, 3 to 4 minutes. Serve immediately.

Canadian Bacon, Tomato and Parmesan Panini

The name Canadian bacon is a bit misleading, as this lean smoked meat more closely resembles ham than regular bacon. Grilling it adds a slight caramelized flavor to the sandwich.

Serves 2

Tips

Canadian bacon costs more than regular bacon, but is leaner and precooked, which means less shrinkage.

During tomato season, take advantage of the numerous varieties available.

Try a variety of greens in this sandwich, such as spinach, romaine, butter or curly leaf.

Use your favorite vinaigrette or whatever is handy in your refrigerator.

Preheat panini grill to high

4	slices Canadian bacon	4
4	slices Italian bread (1-inch/2.5 cm thick slices)	4
1 tbsp	olive oil	15 mL
4	thin slices tomato	4
½ cup	arugula	125 mL
2 tbsp	Basic Vinaigrette (see recipe, page 234)	25 mL
¼ cup	shaved Parmesan cheese	50 mL

1. Arrange bacon on bottom grill plate, close the top plate and cook until crispy, 1 to 2 minutes. Remove and set aside. Wipe grill plates clean.

2. Brush one side of each bread slice with oil. Place two slices on a work surface, oiled side down, and evenly layer with bacon, tomato and arugula. Drizzle with vinaigrette and sprinkle with cheese. Cover with top halves, oiled side up, and press gently to pack.

3. Place sandwiches in grill, close the top plate and cook until golden brown, 3 to 4 minutes. Serve immediately.

Bacon, Smoked Gouda and Tomato Panini

The nutty Gouda melts beautifully, binding together the tomato and bacon for an upscale grilled cheese sandwich.

Serves 2

Tips

Serve this sandwich with a good beer or red wine.

Gouda is perfect for panini — and fondues — because of its excellent melting properties. Edam is similar, and would make a good substitute.

Preheat panini grill to high

4	slices French bread (1-inch/2.5 cm thick slices)	4
1 tbsp	olive oil	15 mL
2 tbsp	mayonnaise	25 mL
2 tbsp	honey mustard	25 mL
3 oz	smoked Gouda cheese, thinly sliced	90 g
8	slices bacon, cooked crisp	8
4	thin slices tomato	4
Pinch	salt	Pinch
Pinch	freshly ground black pepper	Pinch

1. Brush one side of each bread slice with oil. Place on a work surface, oiled side down, and spread mayonnaise over bottom halves. Spread mustard over top halves. On bottom halves, evenly layer with cheese, bacon and tomato. Sprinkle with salt and pepper. Cover with top halves and press gently to pack.

2. Place sandwiches in grill, close the top plate and cook until golden brown, 3 to 4 minutes. Serve immediately.

Bacon, Tomato and Spinach Panini

I love the classic BLT, but when I replaced the lettuce with spinach and added provolone, I loved it even more.

Serves 2

Tip

Provolone is a smoked curd cheese originally made from buffalo milk but now usually made from cow's milk. Aged provolone can be used for grating.

Variation

Adding sautéed mushrooms to this panini gives it a completely different flavor, almost like a whole other recipe.

Preheat panini grill to high

4	slices sourdough bread (½-inch/1 cm thick slices)	4
1 tbsp	butter, melted	15 mL
1 tbsp	mayonnaise	15 mL
2 oz	provolone cheese, thinly sliced	60 g
6	slices thick-cut bacon, cooked crisp	6
4	thin slices tomato	4
½ cup	baby spinach leaves	125 mL
Pinch	salt	Pinch
Pinch	freshly ground black pepper	Pinch

1. Brush one side of each bread slice with butter. Place on a work surface, buttered side down, and spread with mayonnaise. On bottom halves, evenly layer with cheese, bacon, tomato and spinach. Sprinkle with salt and pepper. Cover with top halves and press gently to pack.

2. Place sandwiches in grill, close the top plate and cook until golden brown, 3 to 4 minutes. Serve immediately.

Bacon, Spinach and Hard-Boiled Egg Panini

The hard-boiled egg might make you think of this as a breakfast or brunch panini, but I enjoy it at any time of the day, and it's packed with iron and protein!

Serves 2

Tip

Fresh fruit and yogurt will round out this meal, especially if it's the first meal of the day.

Variations

For a leaner sandwich, use 4 slices of Canadian bacon.

Substitute English muffins or sliced sourdough bread for the ciabatta rolls.

Preheat panini grill to high

2	ciabatta rolls, split	2
3 tbsp	olive oil, divided	45 mL
8	slices bacon, cooked crisp	8
2	hard-boiled eggs, sliced	2
1 cup	baby spinach leaves	250 mL
½ cup	sliced red onion	125 mL
½ cup	crumbled feta cheese	125 mL
2 tbsp	balsamic vinegar	25 mL
Pinch	salt	Pinch
Pinch	freshly ground black pepper	Pinch

1. Place rolls, cut side down, on a work surface and brush crusts with 1 tbsp (15 mL) of the oil. Turn rolls over and, on bottom halves, evenly layer with bacon, eggs, spinach, onion and feta. Drizzle with vinegar and the remaining oil, and sprinkle with salt and pepper. Cover with top halves and press gently to pack.

2. Place sandwiches in grill, close the top plate and cook until golden brown, 3 to 4 minutes. Serve immediately.

Bacon, Blue Cheese and Sweet Onion Panini

I love the flavor combination of the crisp bacon and the tangy, almost nutty, blue cheese. Choose the sweetest onion you can find for this rewarding panini.

Serves 2

Tip

You can always add more onion, or take some away — suit yourself and design your own panini.

Preheat panini grill to high

3 tbsp	olive oil, divided	45 mL
4	thin slices sweet onion, separated into rings	2
Pinch	salt	Pinch
Pinch	freshly ground black pepper	Pinch
4	slices sourdough bread (½-inch/1 cm thick slices)	4
6	slices thick-cut bacon, cooked crisp	6
¼ cup	crumbled blue cheese	50 mL

1. In a skillet, heat 1 tbsp (15 mL) of the oil over medium-high heat. Add onion and sauté until tender, 7 to 9 minutes. Sprinkle with salt and pepper.

2. Brush one side of each bread slice with the remaining oil. Place two slices on a work surface, oiled side down, and evenly layer with onion, bacon and blue cheese. Cover with top halves, oiled side up, and press gently to pack.

3. Place sandwiches in grill, close the top plate and cook until golden brown, 3 to 4 minutes. Serve immediately.

Smashed White Bean, Avocado and Bacon Panini

I love the savory flavor combination in this panini: white kidney beans, smashed to a spreadable consistency, layered with bacon and fresh cucumber, red onion and avocado — it will tantalize your taste buds with each delicious bite.

Serves 2

Tip

If you happen to have leftover smashed beans, spread them atop grilled bread slices and sprinkle with diced bacon and chopped onion for perfect bruschetta. Serve with a crisp wine as an easy hors d'oeuvre.

Variations

For a meatier panini, add sliced or shaved turkey or chicken.

I love the simple white bean, but any type of bean will certainly work. For a different flair, use black beans spiked with a bit of chili powder and cumin.

Preheat panini grill to high

1	can (14 to 19 oz/398 to 540 mL) white kidney beans, drained and rinsed	1
2 tbsp	olive oil, divided	25 mL
Pinch	salt	Pinch
Pinch	freshly ground black pepper	Pinch
Pinch	garlic powder	Pinch
2	ciabatta rolls, split	2
6	thin slices cucumber	6
4	slices bacon, cooked crisp	4
4	thin slices red onion	4
1	avocado, thinly sliced	1

1. In a bowl, combine beans, 1 tbsp (15 mL) of the oil, salt, pepper and garlic powder. Using a potato masher or a fork, mash the bean mixture. Set aside.

2. Place rolls, cut side down, on a work surface and brush crusts with the remaining oil. Turn rolls over and spread bean mixture over bottom halves. Evenly layer with cucumber, bacon, onion and avocado. Cover with top halves and press gently to pack.

3. Place sandwiches in grill, close the top plate and cook until golden brown, 3 to 4 minutes. Serve immediately.

Deli Counter Panini

Panini Dippers

I love these garlicky, cheesy appetizers or snacks — which taste like fried cheese sticks, but with much less fat — dipped in warm marinara sauce.

**Serves 2
as an appetizer**

Tips

Cut these dippers into fun shapes for the kids.

For maximum freshness, grate Parmesan directly from the block or wedge. It's excellent on salads, pasta dishes, omelets and rice dishes. Sliced Parmesan is great as an appetizer, snack or dessert when paired with fruit or crackers.

Preheat panini grill to high

¼ cup	freshly grated Parmesan cheese	50 mL
¼ cup	butter, softened	50 mL
¼ tsp	garlic salt	1 mL
¼ tsp	dried parsley	1 mL
Pinch	freshly ground black pepper	Pinch
4	slices sourdough bread (½-inch/1 cm slices)	4
4 oz	Swiss cheese, thinly sliced	125 g
	Heated marinara sauce	

1. In a bowl, combine Parmesan, butter, garlic salt and parsley.

2. Place bread on a work surface and spread each slice with Parmesan mixture. Turn two slices over and evenly layer with Swiss cheese. Cover with top halves, buttered side up, and press gently to pack.

3. Place sandwiches in grill, close the top plate and cook until golden brown, 3 to 4 minutes. Cut each panini into quarters and serve immediately with marinara sauce for dipping.

Cheddar, Ham and Apple Panini (page 147)

Bacon, Spinach and Hard-Boiled Egg Panini (page 156)

Smashed White Bean, Avocado
and Bacon Panini (page 158)

Ham, Turkey, Avocado and Alfalfa Sprout Panini (page 163)

Salami and Fontina Croissants (page 168)

Muffuletta Panini (page 177)

Hawaiian Chicken Panini (page 185)

Spicy Barbecue Steak Panini with Crispy Onions (page 190)

Spice-It-Up Chicken and Ham Panini

In this panini, ham, chicken and jalapeño peppers are perfectly balanced with Cheddar cheese and barbecue sauce.

Serves 2

Variations

Substitute freshly baked sourdough bread for the bolillo rolls.

Add thinly sliced red onion with the jalapeño.

Preheat panini grill to high

2	bolillo rolls (see tip, page 120), split	2
1 tbsp	butter, melted	15 mL
2 oz	deli smoked ham, thinly sliced	60 g
4 oz	grilled chicken, thinly sliced	125 g
½ cup	Chipotle Barbecue Sauce (see recipe, page 245)	125 mL
½ cup	shredded Cheddar cheese	125 mL
8	slices drained pickled jalapeño pepper	8

1. Place rolls, cut side down, on a work surface and brush crusts with butter. Turn rolls over and, on bottom halves, evenly layer with ham and chicken. Drizzle with barbecue sauce and top with cheese and jalapeño. Cover with top halves and press gently to pack.

2. Place sandwiches in grill, close the top plate and cook until golden brown, 3 to 4 minutes. Serve immediately.

Classic Club Panini

The classic club sandwich is stacked tall with flavor; I have pressed it into a panini but kept all the flavor!

Serves 2

Tip
When lowering the top plate, be especially careful: this sandwich is packed with ingredients.

Variation
Although white bread is the traditional choice for a club sandwich, feel free to substitute a wheat bread variety for the added nutrients.

Preheat panini grill to high

4	slices country-style white bread (½-inch/1 cm thick slices)	4
1 tbsp	butter, melted	15 mL
1 tbsp	mayonnaise	15 mL
2 oz	deli smoked turkey, thinly sliced	60 g
2 oz	deli smoked ham, thinly sliced	60 g
1 oz	Swiss cheese, thinly sliced	30 g
1 oz	Cheddar cheese, thinly sliced	30 g
4	slices bacon, cooked crisp	4
4	thin slices tomato	4
½ cup	shredded iceberg lettuce	125 mL
Pinch	freshly ground black pepper	Pinch
Pinch	dried oregano	Pinch

1. Brush one side of each bread slice with butter. Place on a work surface, buttered side down, and spread with mayonnaise. On bottom halves, evenly layer with turkey, ham, Swiss, Cheddar, bacon, tomato and lettuce. Sprinkle with pepper and oregano. Cover with top halves and press gently to pack.

2. Place sandwiches in grill, close the top plate and cook until golden brown, 3 to 4 minutes. Serve immediately.

Ham, Turkey, Avocado and Alfalfa Sprout Panini

This recipe was inspired by my dear friend and colleague Itza Gutierrez, who loves the combination of avocado and alfalfa sprouts. Add melted Swiss cheese, and you have one incredible sandwich.

Serves 2

Tips

Avocado and alfalfa sprouts are a wonderful combination on many savory dishes and add so much to a simple sandwich or salad.

Variation

This sandwich can quickly go vegetarian if you omit the ham and turkey. Add a thin slice of firm tofu for protein.

Preheat panini grill to high

4	slices sourdough bread (½-inch/1 cm thick slices)	4
1 tbsp	butter, melted	15 mL
1 tbsp	spicy mustard	15 mL
2 oz	Swiss cheese, thinly sliced	60 g
1 oz	deli baked ham, thinly sliced	30 g
1 oz	deli baked turkey, thinly sliced	30 g
1	small avocado, thinly sliced	1
½ cup	alfalfa sprouts	125 mL
Pinch	salt	Pinch
Pinch	freshly ground black pepper	Pinch

1. Brush one side of each bread slice with butter. Place two slices on a work surface, buttered side down, and spread with mustard. Evenly layer with cheese, ham, turkey, avocado and sprouts. Sprinkle with salt and pepper. Cover with top halves, buttered side up, and press gently to pack.

2. Place sandwiches in grill, close the top plate and cook until golden brown, 3 to 4 minutes. Serve immediately.

The All-American

This panini version of a traditional sandwich is packed with three deli meats — ham, turkey and roast beef — for flavor that cannot be beat.

Serves 2

Tip

Serve with kettle potato chips, dill pickles and ice-cold soda.

Variation

Use deli mustard instead of, or in addition to, the mayonnaise.

Preheat panini grill to high

2	hoagie buns, split	2
1 tbsp	olive oil	15 mL
¼ cup	mayonnaise	50 mL
2 oz	provolone cheese, thinly sliced	60 g
2 oz	deli smoked ham, thinly sliced	60 g
2 oz	deli oven-roasted turkey, thinly sliced	60 g
2 oz	deli roast beef, thinly sliced	60 g
6	thin slices tomato	6
½ cup	shredded iceberg lettuce	125 mL
Pinch	dried oregano	Pinch
Pinch	salt	Pinch
Pinch	freshly ground black pepper	Pinch

1. Place buns, cut side down, on a work surface and brush crusts with oil. Turn buns over and spread with mayonnaise. On bottom halves, evenly layer with cheese, ham, turkey, beef, tomato and lettuce. Sprinkle with oregano, salt and pepper. Cover with top halves and press gently to pack.

2. Place sandwiches in grill, close the top plate and cook until golden brown, 3 to 4 minutes. Serve immediately.

Pepperoni and Cheese Panini

My family makes a wonderful version of pepperoni cheese bread, so we made it into a panini.

Serves 2

Tip

I love the grainy texture and the sharp, pungent flavor of Pecorino Romano cheese, which is in the hard cheese category. Use a vegetable peeler to shave off thin slices of cheese to use in panini, or grate it to sprinkle over a salad or to use in cooking.

Preheat panini grill to high

2	ciabatta rolls, split	2
1 tbsp	olive oil	15 mL
4 oz	mozzarella cheese, thinly sliced	125 g
2 oz	Pecorino Romano cheese, thinly sliced	60 g
1 oz	pepperoni, thinly sliced	30 g
Pinch	dried oregano	Pinch
Pinch	salt	Pinch
Pinch	freshly ground black pepper	Pinch

1. Place rolls, cut side down, on a work surface and brush crusts with oil. Turn rolls over and, on bottom halves, evenly layer with mozzarella, Pecorino Romano and pepperoni. Sprinkle with oregano, salt and pepper. Cover with top halves and press gently to pack.

2. Place sandwiches in grill, close the top plate and cook until golden brown, 3 to 4 minutes. Serve immediately.

The Tiffany

I have discovered a small neighborhood pizza place I adore. When they see me walk in, they never have to ask for my order. I've put my favorite pizza toppings into this sandwich, and I present to you my signature panini. I hope you enjoy it as much as I do.

Serves 2

Variations

If you prefer, substitute pickled pepperoncini peppers for the jalapeños.

I have made this with a mixture of brine-cured olives, with excellent results.

Preheat panini grill to high

2	ciabatta rolls, split	2
1 tbsp	olive oil	15 mL
½ cup	pizza sauce or marinara sauce	125 mL
2 oz	mozzarella cheese, thinly sliced	60 g
1 oz	pepperoni, thinly sliced	30 g
¼ cup	sliced drained kalamata olives	50 mL
¼ cup	crumbled feta cheese	50 mL
¼ cup	sliced drained pickled jalapeño peppers	50 mL

1. Place rolls, cut side down, on a work surface and brush crusts with oil. Turn rolls over and spread with pizza sauce. On bottom halves, evenly layer with mozzarella, pepperoni, olives, feta and jalapeños. Cover with top halves and press gently to pack.

2. Place sandwiches in grill, close the top plate and cook until golden brown, 3 to 4 minutes. Serve immediately.

Summer Sausage
and Pepper Jack Panini

A dear friend who grew up in the Midwest used to devour summer sausage sandwiches, so we heated the ingredients in a panini. The tartness of the mustard, the kick of the pepper Jack cheese and the sweet heat of the pepperoncini peppers make for a lively sandwich.

**Serves 2
as an appetizer**

Tip

Summer sausage is any type of sausage that doesn't need refrigeration.

Preheat panini grill to high

4	slices sourdough bread (1/2-inch/1 cm thick slices)	4
1 tbsp	olive oil	15 mL
2 tbsp	deli mustard	25 mL
3 oz	summer sausage, thinly sliced	90 g
2 oz	pepper Jack cheese, thinly sliced	60 g
2	pickled pepperoncini peppers, drained and thinly sliced	2

1. Brush one side of each bread slice with oil. Place on a work surface, oiled side down, and spread with mustard. On bottom halves, evenly layer with sausage, cheese and pepperoncini. Cover with top halves and press gently to pack.

2. Place sandwiches in grill, close the top plate and cook until golden brown, 3 to 4 minutes. Serve immediately.

Salami and Fontina Croissants

When you're in the mood for a calorie splurge, buttery croissants pair well with fontina, salami, arugula and Parmesan.

Serves 2 as an appetizer

Tips

I love using freshly shaved Parmesan cheese in panini — and it's also a favorite snack, combined with a velvety glass of Zinfandel.

Croissants are made with butter spread between each delectable layer of pastry dough, so there's no need to butter or oil the crusts.

Variation

To control fat and cut calories in this recipe, use French or Italian bread instead of croissants

Preheat panini grill to high

2	croissants, split	2
2 oz	fontina cheese, thinly sliced	60 g
2 oz	salami, thinly sliced	60 g
½ cup	arugula	125 mL
½ cup	shaved or freshly grated Parmesan cheese	125 mL

1. Place croissants, crust side down, on a work surface. On bottom halves, evenly layer with fontina, salami, arugula and Parmesan. Cover with top halves and press gently to pack.

2. Place sandwiches in grill, close the top plate and cook until golden brown, 3 to 4 minutes. Serve immediately.

Salami and Gouda Panini

Gouda's nutty flavor is great melted with fresh tomato, arugula and thinly sliced salami. Enjoy this sandwich with a glass of red wine.

Serves 2

Tips

Alternate layers of salami and Gouda for a true melding of the flavors.

I love a good-quality balsamic vinegar drizzled on just about anything, especially a sandwich like this. Sprinkle it on before covering with the top halves.

Preheat panini grill to high

2	ciabatta rolls, split	2
1 tbsp	olive oil	15 mL
2 oz	Gouda cheese, thinly sliced	60 g
2 oz	salami, thinly sliced	60 g
4	thin slices tomato	4
½ cup	arugula	125 mL
Pinch	salt	Pinch
Pinch	freshly ground black pepper	Pinch

1. Place rolls, cut side down, on a work surface and brush crusts with oil. Turn rolls over and, on bottom halves, evenly layer with cheese, salami, tomato and arugula. Sprinkle with salt and pepper. Cover with top halves and press gently to pack.

2. Place sandwiches in grill, close the top plate and cook until golden brown, 3 to 4 minutes. Serve immediately.

Salami, Mozzarella and Fontina Panini

This panini melts two fabulous Italian cheeses with the flavor of salami. Add the bite of pepperoncini, and you have an amazing sandwich, hot off the panini grill.

Serves 2

Tip

If you can't find aïoli and don't have time to make it, substitute mayonnaise.

Variation

Create your own variation by pairing the salami of your choice with any cheese you enjoy.

Preheat panini grill to high

4	slices Italian bread (½-inch/1 cm thick slices)	4
1 tbsp	olive oil	15 mL
1 tbsp	aïoli (store-bought or see recipe, page 240)	15 mL
2 oz	salami, thinly sliced	60 g
2 oz	mozzarella cheese, thinly sliced	60 g
2 oz	fontina cheese, thinly sliced	60 g
2	pickled pepperoncini peppers, drained and thinly sliced	2

1. Brush one side of each bread slice with oil. Place on a work surface, oiled side down, and spread with aïoli. On bottom halves, evenly layer with salami, mozzarella, fontina and pepperoncini. Cover with top halves and press gently to pack.

2. Place sandwiches in grill, close the top plate and cook until golden brown, 3 to 4 minutes. Serve immediately.

Double Cheese and Salami Panini

Doubling the cheese makes for a perfect panini — very gooey, but wonderful with the salami of your choice.

**Serves 2
as an appetizer**

Tip

I enjoy the peppery flavor of arugula in panini recipes. This green is highly perishable, so make sure to keep it in the refrigerator and use it within 2 days of purchase.

Preheat panini grill to high

4	slices sourdough bread (½-inch/1 cm thick slices)	4
1 tbsp	olive oil	15 mL
2 oz	salami, thinly sliced	60 g
2 oz	smoked Gouda cheese, thinly sliced	60 g
½ cup	arugula	125 mL
¼ cup	shaved Parmesan cheese	50 mL

1. Brush one side of each bread slice with oil. Place two slices on a work surface, oiled side down, and evenly layer with salami, Gouda, arugula and Parmesan. Cover with top halves, oiled side up, and press gently to pack.

2. Place sandwiches in grill, close the top plate and cook until golden brown, 3 to 4 minutes. Serve immediately.

Salami, Prosciutto and Roasted Pepper Panini

This sandwich is so sophisticated, yet so simple to prepare. Have the deli slice the prosciutto and the salami paper-thin.

Serves 2

Tip

If you're not up to roasting red peppers yourself, you can find bottled roasted red peppers in the supermarket. Drain the peppers and pat them dry before slicing and measuring.

Preheat panini grill to high

2	Italian rolls, split	2
1 tbsp	olive oil	15 mL
2 oz	salami, sliced paper-thin	60 g
2 oz	prosciutto, sliced paper-thin	60 g
2 oz	mozzarella cheese, thinly sliced	60 g
1/3 cup	sliced roasted red bell pepper	75 mL

1. Place rolls, cut side down, on a work surface and brush crusts with oil. Turn rolls over and, on bottom halves, evenly layer with salami, prosciutto, cheese and roasted pepper. Cover with top halves and press gently to pack.

2. Place sandwiches in grill, close the top plate and cook until golden brown, 3 to 4 minutes. Serve immediately.

Prosciutto, Salami and Provolone Panini

Incredible flavor results when you combine thinly sliced prosciutto and salami with a melting of provolone cheese.

Serves 2

Tips

Pepperoncini peppers are so good, especially in this recipe. I enjoy biting off the ends and sprinkling the briny juices over the panini filling. I do this with salads and pizzas too. Look for pepperoncini in the condiment section of your supermarket.

Aïoli is a garlic-flavored mayonnaise used in Provençal cuisine.

Preheat panini grill to high

2	4-inch (10 cm) focaccia, halved horizontally	2
1 tbsp	olive oil	15 mL
1 tbsp	aïoli (store-bought or see recipe, page 240)	15 mL
2 oz	salami, sliced paper-thin	60 g
2 oz	prosciutto, sliced paper-thin	60 g
2 oz	sharp provolone cheese, thinly sliced	60 g
4	thin slices red onion	4
2	pickled pepperoncini peppers, drained and thinly sliced	2

1. Place focaccia, cut side down, on a work surface and brush crusts with oil. Turn focaccia over and spread with aïoli. On bottom halves, evenly layer with salami, prosciutto, cheese, onion and pepperoncini. Cover with top halves and press gently to pack.

2. Place sandwiches in grill, close the top plate and cook until golden brown, 3 to 4 minutes. Serve immediately.

Soppressata and Sharp Cheddar Panini

Although I have not traveled to Italy, I trust I will venture there in the future to enjoy the countryside and experience the fabulous panini. Enjoy this panini with flavorful soppressata, an Italian sausage found in supermarkets.

Serves 2

Tip

Look for soppressata — a pressed Italian sausage — at your supermarket's deli counter. If you cannot find it, you can substitute any other Italian sausage.

Variation

Provolone and mozzarella are good substitutions for the Cheddar.

Preheat panini grill to high

4	slices sourdough bread (½-inch/1 cm thick slices)	4
1 tbsp	olive oil	15 mL
2 tbsp	mayonnaise	25 mL
2 oz	soppressata or hard salami, thinly sliced	60 g
2 oz	sharp (old) Cheddar cheese, thinly sliced	60 g
4	thin slices tomato	4
4	thin slices red onion	4
2	red-tipped or romaine lettuce leaves	2
2 tbsp	Basic Vinaigrette (see recipe, page 234)	25 mL
Pinch	salt	Pinch
Pinch	freshly ground black pepper	Pinch

1. Brush one side of each bread slice with oil. Place on a work surface, oiled side down, and spread with mayonnaise. On bottom halves, evenly layer with soppressata, cheese, tomato, onion and lettuce. Drizzle with vinaigrette and sprinkle with salt and pepper. Cover with top halves and press gently to pack.

2. Place sandwiches in grill, close the top plate and cook until golden brown, 3 to 4 minutes. Serve immediately.

Fried Bologna, American Cheese and Arugula Panini

As a child, I loved fried bologna sandwiches on white bread with Miracle Whip salad dressing. Gone are those days; I now enjoy a grown-up fried bologna sandwich.

Serves 2

Tip

Grilling bologna works well in the panini maker, because the top plate keeps the bologna from curling.

Variation

White American cheese is the perfect choice for me in this recipe, but Cheddar would make a great substitution.

Preheat panini grill to high

2	slices bologna (each about ¼ inch/0.5 cm thick)	2
4	slices sourdough bread (½-inch/1 cm thick slices)	4
1 tbsp	butter, melted	15 mL
1 tbsp	spicy mustard	15 mL
2 oz	white American cheese, thinly sliced	60 g
½ cup	arugula	125 mL

1. Arrange bologna on bottom grill plate, close the top plate and cook until browned, 1 to 2 minutes. Remove and keep warm. Wipe grill plates clean.

2. Brush one side of each bread slice with butter. Place on a work surface, buttered side down, and spread with mustard. On bottom halves, evenly layer with bologna, cheese and arugula. Cover with top halves and press gently to pack.

3. Place sandwiches in grill, close the top plate and cook until golden brown, 3 to 4 minutes. Serve immediately.

The Italian

True Italian ingredients adorn this authentic panini. Someday I will travel to Italy and experience a slice of heaven, but until then I have my version of the Italian panini.

Serves 2

Tip

Look for mortadella and capicola at your supermarket's deli counter or at specialty food markets. Mortadella typically has a garlic flavor, which adds so much to panini recipes. Capicola is dry-cured whole and is more expensive than most salami — but it's worth it!

Preheat panini grill to high

2	ciabatta rolls, split	2
1 tbsp	olive oil	15 mL
2 tbsp	Basil Mayonnaise (see recipe, page 236)	25 mL
2 oz	provolone cheese, thinly sliced	60 g
2 oz	hard salami, thinly sliced	60 g
2 oz	mortadella, thinly sliced	60 g
2 oz	capicola, thinly sliced	60 g
4	thin tomato slices	4
¼ cup	sliced red onion	50 mL

1. Place rolls, cut side down, on a work surface and brush crusts with oil. Turn rolls over and spread with mayonnaise. On bottom halves, evenly layer with cheese, salami, mortadella, capicola, tomato and red onion. Cover with top halves and press gently to pack.

2. Place sandwiches in grill, close the top plate and cook until golden brown, 3 to 4 minutes. Serve immediately.

Muffuletta Panini

The classic muffuletta recipe, so popular in New Orleans, is distinguished by its olive salad topping. I've chosen to use my homemade olive tapenade, but you could make your own olive salad or purchase one at your supermarket's deli counter.

Serves 2

Variation

Muffuletta is traditionally made with Italian bread, but focaccia also works well.

Preheat panini grill to high

2	round Italian rolls, split	2
1 tbsp	olive oil	15 mL
½ cup	olive tapenade (store-bought or see recipe, page 242)	125 mL
¼ cup	shaved Parmesan cheese	50 mL
2 oz	capicola, thinly sliced	60 g
2 oz	mozzarella cheese, thinly sliced	60 g
2 oz	mortadella, thinly sliced	60 g
2 oz	provolone cheese, thinly sliced	60 g
Pinch	dried basil	Pinch
Pinch	dried oregano	Pinch

1. Brush both the cut and crust sides of rolls with oil. Place on a work surface, crust side down, and spread tapenade over bottom halves. On top of the tapenade, evenly layer, in this order, Parmesan, capicola, mozzarella, mortadella and provolone. Sprinkle with basil and oregano. Cover with top halves and press gently to pack.

2. Place sandwiches in grill, close the top plate and cook until golden brown, 3 to 4 minutes. Serve immediately.

French Dip Panini with Au Jus Dipping Sauce

Each time I have a meal that includes a sauce, I cannot wait to soak up every last bit on my plate with a crusty roll or a slice of warm bread. Keeping that in mind, it seems natural to include my version of a French dip sandwich, warmed until crisp in my panini grill. The sauce is so rich, and gives such amazing dimension to this recipe. Enjoy every last morsel!

Serves 2

Tips

You can choose to use either shallot or garlic, but I love the combination of flavors. Never let garlic burn, as the flavor will become bitter.

French dips are typically served on baguettes, but I love the texture of a hoagie or submarine roll when it's pressed in the panini grill. Sourdough bread, fresh from the oven or your local bakery, would also be terrific with this recipe.

Serve with a fresh tomato, basil and buffalo mozzarella salad, drizzled with a good-quality balsamic vinegar and a sprinkling of kosher salt and freshly ground black pepper.

Preheat panini grill to high

1 tbsp	butter	15 mL
1 tbsp	chopped shallot	15 mL
1 tbsp	minced garlic	15 mL
1½ tsp	all-purpose flour	7 mL
1	can (10 oz/284 mL) beef consommé	1
2	submarine or hoagie rolls, split	2
1 tbsp	butter, melted	15 mL
4 oz	deli roast beef, thinly sliced	125 g
2 oz	provolone cheese, thinly sliced	60 g
	Salt and freshly ground black pepper	

1. In a small skillet, melt 1 tbsp (15 mL) butter over medium heat. Add shallot and garlic; sauté until aromatic, 1 to 2 minutes. Sprinkle with flour and sauté for 1 minute. Gradually whisk in consommé until flour is dissolved. Bring to a boil, then reduce heat to low and let simmer gently until ready to serve.

2. Place rolls, cut side down, on a work surface and brush crusts with melted butter. Turn rolls over and, on bottom halves, evenly layer with roast beef and cheese. Sprinkle with salt and pepper to taste. Cover with top halves and press gently to pack.

3. Place sandwiches in grill, close the top plate and cook until golden brown, 3 to 4 minutes. Serve immediately, with warm dipping sauce on the side.

Leftovers Panini

Chicken Salad Panini

Chicken salad is so fresh, so good — just perfect packed into grilled bread. I also enjoy grilling a single slice of bread, placing a mound of chicken on top and eating it with a fork.

Serves 2

Tip

This panini works well with any chicken salad recipe, whether it's a savory version with dill pickles, onions and mayonnaise or a sweeter version with green and red grapes, apples and walnuts.

Preheat panini grill to high

4	slices whole wheat bread (½-inch/1 cm thick slices)	4
1 tbsp	butter, melted	15 mL
1 cup	leftover chicken salad	250 mL

1. Brush one side of each bread slice with butter. Place two slices on a work surface, buttered side down, and spread chicken salad over bottom halves. Cover with top halves, buttered side up, and press gently to pack.

2. Place sandwiches in grill, close the top plate so that it barely touches the sandwiches and cook until golden brown, 3 to 4 minutes. Serve immediately.

Clubhouse Chicken Panini

For this recipe, I transferred the ingredients of a favorite sandwich, the club, and pressed them in a panini. I left out the additional bread slice, as I did not miss it, but indulged in a grilled chicken breast.

Serves 2

Variations

Substitute pitas or another type of flatbread for the sourdough.

Add sliced cucumber with the tomato.

Preheat panini grill to high

4	slices sourdough bread (½-inch/1 cm thick slices)	4
1 tbsp	butter, melted	15 mL
4 oz	leftover grilled chicken breast (about 1 small), thinly sliced	125 g
2 tbsp	ranch dressing or mayonnaise	25 mL
4	thin slices tomato	4
3	slices bacon, cooked crisp and crumbled	3
½ cup	shredded Cheddar cheese	125 mL

1. Brush one side of each bread slice with butter. Place two slices on a work surface, buttered side down, and evenly layer with chicken. Drizzle with ranch dressing, then evenly layer with tomato, bacon and cheese. Cover with top halves, buttered side up, and press gently to pack.

2. Place sandwiches in grill, close the top plate and cook until golden brown, 3 to 4 minutes. Serve immediately.

Philly Chicken Panini

This panini is inspired by a Philly chicken sandwich I had several years ago in Philadelphia. All that's missing is the ambience of Pennsylvania.

Serves 2

Tip

When I don't have leftovers, I often use shaved deli chicken breast.

Variation

As a substitute for the Cheddar cheese, shredded mozzarella is great with the sautéed onion and peppers.

Preheat panini grill to high

2 tbsp	olive oil, divided	25 mL
¼ cup	finely chopped white onion	50 mL
¼ cup	diced red bell pepper	50 mL
¼ cup	diced green bell pepper	50 mL
4	slices Italian bread (½-inch/1 cm thick slices)	4
4 oz	leftover grilled chicken breast (about 1 small), thinly sliced	125 g
½ cup	shredded Cheddar cheese	125 mL
¼ cup	sliced drained pickled pepperoncini pepper	50 mL

1. In a skillet, heat 2 tsp (10 mL) of the oil over medium-high heat. Add onion, red pepper and green pepper; sauté until softened, 7 to 9 minutes. Remove from heat and keep warm.

2. Brush one side of each bread slice with the remaining oil. Place two slices on a work surface, oiled side down, and evenly layer with chicken, onion mixture, cheese and pepperoncini. Cover with top halves, oiled side up, and press gently to pack.

3. Place sandwiches in grill, close the top plate and cook until golden brown, 3 to 4 minutes. Serve immediately.

Buffalo Blue Chicken Panini

Buffalo wings are a hit everywhere, with their fiery flavor that begs for blue cheese dressing. I took these flavors and made a flavorful grilled sandwich.

Serves 2

Tip
Serve with celery sticks and blue cheese dressing.

Variation
Caramelized onions are wonderful in this panini, but sliced red onions add a bit of crunch and a different flavor.

Preheat panini grill to high

2	ciabatta rolls, split	2
1 tbsp	butter, melted	15 mL
8 oz	leftover grilled chicken breast (about 2 small), thinly sliced	250 g
⅓ cup	Chipotle Barbecue Sauce (see recipe, page 245)	75 mL
½ cup	Caramelized Onions (see recipe, page 248)	125 mL
½ cup	crumbled blue cheese	125 mL

1. Place rolls, cut side down, on a work surface and brush crusts with butter. Turn rolls over and, on bottom halves evenly layer with chicken. Drizzle with barbecue sauce, then evenly layer with caramelized onions and blue cheese. Cover with top halves and press gently to pack.

2. Place sandwiches in grill, close the top plate and cook until golden brown, 3 to 4 minutes. Serve immediately.

Chicken Salsa Quesadillas

Flour tortillas encase grilled chicken, fresh avocado, plum tomato and a bit of sauce made from condiments you may already have in your refrigerator.

Serves 2

Tip
Try tortillas flavored with chipotle peppers, sun-dried tomatoes, spinach or herbs.

Variation
Add black olives, black beans and chopped cilantro.

Preheat panini grill to high

¼ cup	ranch dressing	50 mL
2 tbsp	good-quality salsa	25 mL
2	8- to 10-inch (20 to 25 cm) flour tortillas	2
2 tsp	butter, melted	10 mL
4 oz	leftover grilled chicken breast (about 1 small), thinly sliced	125 g
1	small avocado, thinly sliced	1
1	plum (Roma) tomato, thinly sliced	1
½ cup	shredded Monterey Jack cheese	125 mL
	Guacamole, salsa and sour cream	

1. In a bowl, combine ranch dressing and salsa; set aside.

2. Brush one side of each tortilla with butter. Place on a work surface, buttered side down, and evenly layer chicken over half of each tortilla, leaving a ½-inch (1 cm) border around the edges. Drizzle with dressing mixture, then evenly layer with avocado, tomato and cheese. Fold tortillas over filling, pressing gently to pack.

3. Place sandwiches in grill, close the top plate and cook until filling is hot and cheese is melted, 3 to 4 minutes. Cut each sandwich in half and serve immediately with guacamole, salsa and sour cream.

Hawaiian Chicken Panini

I encourage you to use fresh pineapple, as once it is grilled the natural sugar will caramelize, giving more depth to the flavor, color and texture. The island flavors of teriyaki, Maui onion and cabbage highlight this recipe.

Serves 2

Tips

For additional flavor, brush the pineapple slices with teriyaki sauce before grilling.

Look in your supermarket's freezer section for fully cooked grilled chicken, which is great for panini recipes. I prefer slicing it for an easier bite.

Variation

Sprinkle chopped toasted peanuts on top of the cabbage for added crunch and a nutty flavor.

Preheat panini grill to high

2	slices fresh pineapple (about 1/4 inch/0.5 cm thick)	2
2	ciabatta rolls, split	2
1 tbsp	butter, melted	15 mL
1/3 cup	bottled teriyaki glaze	75 mL
8 oz	leftover grilled chicken breast (about 2 small), thinly sliced	250 g
4	thin slices Sweet Maui onion or other sweet onion	4
1/2 cup	shredded napa cabbage	125 mL

1. Arrange pineapple on bottom grill plate, close the top plate and grill until pineapple is tender and grill-marked, 1 to 2 minutes. Remove and keep warm. Wipe grill plates clean.

2. Place rolls, cut side down, on a work surface and brush crusts with butter. Turn rolls over and brush with some of the teriyaki glaze. On bottom halves, evenly layer with chicken, pineapple, onion and cabbage. Drizzle with the remaining teriyaki glaze. Cover with top halves and press gently to pack.

3. Place sandwiches in grill, close the top plate and cook until golden brown, 3 to 4 minutes. Serve immediately.

Chicken Marinara Panini

When I developed this recipe, I had leftover chicken and marinara sauce, so I created this yummy panini with a blend of two Italian cheeses.

Serves 2

Tip
Leftover breaded chicken also works well and gives this panini a different texture.

Preheat panini grill to high

2	4-inch (10 cm) focaccia, halved horizontally	2
1 tbsp	olive oil	15 mL
1 cup	shredded leftover deli rotisserie chicken	250 mL
½ cup	marinara sauce, heated	125 mL
1	small plum (Roma) tomato, thinly sliced	1
½	small green bell pepper, thinly sliced	½
½ cup	shredded mozzarella cheese	125 mL
¼ cup	sliced drained black olives	50 mL
1 tbsp	freshly grated Parmesan cheese	15 mL

1. Place focaccia, cut side down, on a work surface and brush crusts with oil. Turn focaccia over and, on bottom halves, evenly layer with chicken. Drizzle with marinara sauce, then evenly layer with tomato, green pepper, mozzarella, olives and Parmesan. Cover with top halves and press gently to pack.

2. Place sandwiches in grill, close the top plate and cook until golden brown, 3 to 4 minutes. Serve immediately.

Chicken Parmesan Panini

Classic chicken Parmesan — either homemade or leftovers from your favorite Italian eatery — turns into a gourmet panini very quickly and with very little effort.

Serves 2

Tip

If you happen to have leftover garlic bread, use it — it makes for a very authentic chicken Parmesan sandwich!

Preheat panini grill to high

4	slices Italian bread ($\frac{1}{2}$-inch/1 cm thick slices)	4
1 tbsp	olive oil	15 mL
$\frac{1}{2}$ cup	marinara sauce, heated	125 mL
2	leftover cooked breaded chicken breasts, reheated	2
$\frac{1}{2}$ cup	shredded mozzarella cheese	125 mL
$\frac{1}{4}$ cup	freshly grated Parmesan cheese	50 mL

1. Brush one side of each bread slice with oil. Place two slices on a work surface, oiled side down, and spread with half the marinara sauce. Place a chicken breast on each slice and spread with the remaining marinara sauce. Evenly layer with mozzarella and Parmesan. Cover with top halves, oiled side up, and press gently to pack.

2. Place sandwiches in grill, close the top plate and cook until golden brown, 3 to 4 minutes. Serve immediately

Thanksgiving Leftovers Panini

Thanksgiving leftovers are often better than the main meal itself. My family has always served cornbread stuffing, which is amazing in this panini. My sister makes fun of my brother and me, as we always have so much cranberry sauce on our plates, but I just love the tastes of turkey and cranberry together.

Serves 2

Tips

Although I love homemade cranberry sauce, I prefer canned. Either will work in this recipe.

This panini is good any day you have the craving, not just after Thanksgiving. Use 2 oz (60 g) deli roasted turkey breast, thinly sliced.

Preheat panini grill to high

4	slices country-style wheat bread (½-inch/1 cm thick slices)	4
1 tbsp	butter, melted	15 mL
2 tbsp	cranberry sauce	25 mL
½ cup	leftover bread stuffing (preferably cornbread stuffing), reheated	125 mL
2	slices leftover roasted turkey breast	2
¼ cup	leftover turkey gravy, reheated	50 mL

1. Brush one side of each bread slice with butter. Place on a work surface, buttered side down, and spread cranberry sauce over top halves. On bottom halves, evenly layer with stuffing and turkey. Drizzle with gravy. Cover with top halves and press gently to pack.

2. Place sandwiches in grill, close the top plate so that it barely touches the sandwiches and cook until golden brown, 3 to 4 minutes. Serve immediately

Pot Roast Panini

Sunday dinner leftovers easily turn into so many other great recipes, including this panini. I've jazzed it up with a bit of bite, using horseradish mayonnaise and crumbled blue cheese. Cook a larger roast to make sure you have leftovers for this amazing sandwich.

Serves 2

Tips

Use plain mayonnaise if you don't care for the taste of horseradish.

This recipe also works well in hamburger buns.

Preheat panini grill to high

4	slices sourdough bread (½-inch/1 cm thick slices)	4
1 tbsp	butter, melted	15 mL
2 tbsp	Horseradish Mayonnaise (see recipe, page 238)	25 mL
1½ cups	shredded leftover cooked beef pot roast, reheated	375 mL
4	slices red onion	4
2 tbsp	crumbled blue cheese	25 mL

1. Brush one side of each bread slice with butter. Place on a work surface, buttered side down, and spread with mayonnaise. On bottom halves, evenly layer with pot roast, onion and blue cheese. Cover with top halves and press gently to pack.

2. Place sandwiches in grill, close the top plate and cook until golden brown, 3 to 4 minutes. Serve immediately.

Spicy Barbecue Steak Panini with Crispy Onions

Beef combines with spicy barbecue sauce and crisp fried onions to make the perfect panini.

Serves 2

Tips

This recipe is wonderful with or without the fried onions. If you prefer, use sliced or sautéed onions.

To ensure proper internal cooking with a perfect crust on the outside, make sure the oil is heated to 375°F (190°C) before frying the onions.

Preheat panini grill to high
Candy/deep-fry thermometer

	Vegetable oil	
2 cups	all-purpose flour	500 mL
1 tbsp	salt	15 mL
1 tsp	freshly ground black pepper	5 mL
½ tsp	paprika	2 mL
1	large onion, thinly sliced and separated into rings	1
2	hoagie buns, split	2
1 tbsp	butter, melted	15 mL
1 tbsp	mayonnaise	15 mL
4 oz	leftover grilled steak, very thinly sliced (about 6 slices)	125 g
2 oz	smoked Cheddar cheese, thinly sliced	60 g
⅓ cup	Chipotle Barbecue Sauce (see recipe, page 245)	75 mL

1. In a deep, heavy skillet, heat about 2 inches (5 cm) of oil over high heat until it registers 375°F (190°C) on thermometer, about 10 minutes.

2. Meanwhile, in a large bowl, combine flour, salt, pepper and paprika. Add onion and toss to lightly coat, shaking off and discarding excess flour. Carefully transfer onion rings to the hot oil and fry, turning once, until golden brown and crispy, 3 to 5 minutes. Using a slotted spoon, transfer to a plate lined with paper towels and keep warm.

As a true Texan, I love the flavor of chipotle barbecue sauce drizzled on almost anything savory. But feel free to use your favorite sauce.

3. Place buns, cut side down, on a work surface and brush crusts with butter. Turn buns over and spread mayonnaise over bottom halves. Evenly layer with steak, cheese and 1 cup (250 mL) of the fried onions. Drizzle with barbecue sauce. Cover with top halves and press gently to pack.

4. Place sandwiches in grill, close the top plate and cook until golden brown, 3 to 4 minutes. Serve immediately, with the remaining fried onions on the side.

Barbecue Cheese Steak Panini

I like using leftover flank steak on this panini, as the texture and uniform pieces are perfect for sandwiches. You decide whether you want your barbecue sauce to add sweetness, tang or heat.

Serves 2

Variation

Substitute shredded pepper Jack cheese for a bit of heat.

Preheat panini grill to high

2 tbsp	olive oil, divided	25 mL
½	small red onion, thinly sliced	½
½	small green bell pepper, thinly sliced	½
2	sourdough sandwich rolls, split	2
4 oz	leftover grilled steak, thinly sliced (about 6 slices)	125 g
½ cup	barbecue sauce (store-bought or see recipe, page 245)	125 mL
½ cup	shredded provolone cheese	125 mL

1. In a skillet, heat 2 tsp (10 mL) of the oil over medium-high heat. Add onion and green pepper; sauté until softened, 7 to 9 minutes. Remove from heat and keep warm.

2. Place rolls, cut side down, on a work surface and brush crusts with the remaining oil. Turn rolls over and, on bottom halves, evenly layer with steak and onion mixture. Drizzle with barbecue sauce, then evenly layer with cheese. Cover with top halves and press gently to pack.

3. Place sandwiches in grill, close the top plate and cook until golden brown, 3 to 4 minutes. Serve immediately.

Brisket Panini

Large briskets are often cooked with leftovers in mind, and what better way to use them up than in panini?

Serves 2

Tips

In my opinion, brisket calls for pickles. Choose your favorite and serve alongside this panini.

Sandwich rolls would make a denser, heartier panini, good for healthy appetites.

Preheat panini grill to high

¼ cup	mayonnaise	50 mL
2 tbsp	barbecue sauce (store-bought or see recipe, page 245)	25 mL
4	slices country-style white bread (½-inch/1 cm thick slices)	4
1 tbsp	butter, melted	15 mL
6	thin slices leftover smoked beef brisket	90 g
2 oz	Muenster cheese, thinly sliced	60 g
½ cup	baby spinach leaves	125 mL
4	thin slices tomato	4

1. In a bowl, combine mayonnaise and barbecue sauce; set aside.

2. Brush one side of each bread slice with butter. Place on a work surface, buttered side down, and spread with mayonnaise mixture. On bottom halves, evenly layer with brisket, cheese, spinach and tomato. Cover with top halves and press gently to pack.

3. Place sandwiches in grill, close the top plate and cook until golden brown, 3 to 4 minutes. Serve immediately

Steak Gorgonzola Panini

Grilled steak leftovers from a weekend cookout are paired with Gorgonzola, roasted peppers and arugula in this scrumptious panini.

Serves 2

Tips

Steaks cooked rare are perfect for reheating — that way, they're not overcooked for the panini.

If you're in a hurry, just brush with melted butter instead of the garlic butter mixture.

Preheat panini grill to high

3 tbsp	butter, melted	45 mL
2	cloves garlic, finely chopped	2
½ tsp	chopped fresh parsley	2 mL
½ tsp	salt	2 mL
¼ tsp	freshly ground black pepper	1 mL
4	slices French bread (½-inch/1 cm thick slices)	4
4 oz	leftover grilled steak, very thinly sliced (about 6 slices)	125 g
½ cup	arugula	125 mL
⅓ cup	thinly sliced roasted red bell peppers	75 mL
¼ cup	crumbled Gorgonzola cheese	50 mL

1. In a bowl, combine butter, garlic, parsley, salt and pepper.

2. Brush one side of each bread slice with butter mixture. Place two slices on a work surface, buttered side down, and evenly layer with steak, arugula and roasted peppers. Sprinkle with cheese. Cover with top halves, buttered side up, and press gently to pack.

3. Place sandwiches in grill, close the top plate and cook until golden brown, 3 to 4 minutes. Serve immediately.

Beef Fajita Quesadillas

If you're ever in San Antonio, you must dine at my friend Dianna Barrios Trevino's restaurants, Los Barrios and La Hacienda De Los Barrios, where you will find the best Tex-Mex in all of Texas. Dianna helped me develop this panini, which includes ingredients she uses in many of her wonderful dishes.

Serves 2

Tips

Serve with black beans and Spanish rice. Garnish the plate with a lime wedge.

You may be able to find good-quality tomatillo sauce at your local supermarket if you're not up to making your own.

Chihuahua cheese is a wonderful cheese made in the Chihuahua region of Mexico. I love using it in sandwiches, enchiladas and egg dishes. It's also great in fondue recipes and fried.

Variation

This recipe is also great with leftover chicken, pork or shrimp — it's very versatile.

Preheat panini grill to high

¾ cup	diced steak, left over from beef fajitas	175 mL
¼ cup	Tomatillo Sauce (see recipe, page 247)	50 mL
2 tbsp	chopped fresh cilantro	25 mL
2	8- to 10-inch (20 to 25 cm) flour tortillas	2
2 tsp	butter, melted	10 mL
½ cup	shredded Chihuahua or Monterey Jack cheese	125 mL
	Sour cream, guacamole and salsa	

1. In a bowl, combine steak, tomatillo sauce and cilantro; set aside.

2. Brush one side of each tortilla with butter. Place on a work surface, buttered side down, and spoon beef mixture onto half of each tortilla, dividing evenly and leaving a ½-inch (1 cm) border around the edges. Sprinkle each with half the cheese. Fold tortillas over filling, pressing gently to pack.

3. Place sandwiches in grill, close the top plate and cook until filling is hot and cheese is melted, 3 to 4 minutes. Cut each sandwich in half and serve immediately with sour cream, guacamole and salsa.

Beefy Greek Panini

Traditional Greek ingredients accompany grilled steak tucked into flatbread. Creamy tzatziki is the perfect sauce for this panini.

Serves 2

Tips

Fresh homemade tzatziki is perfect, but for convenience, look for it in your supermarket.

Season the feta cheese with chopped fresh basil, diced seeded tomato and freshly ground black pepper.

Preheat panini grill to high

4 oz	leftover grilled steak, thinly sliced (about 6 slices)	125 g
½	small red onion, thinly sliced	½
2 tbsp	Basic Vinaigrette (see recipe, page 234)	25 mL
2	7-inch (18 cm) pitas	2
1 tbsp	olive oil	15 mL
⅓ cup	tzatziki (store-bought or see recipe, page 243)	75 mL
¼ cup	crumbled feta cheese	50 mL

1. In a bowl, toss steak and red onion in vinaigrette; set aside.

2. Brush one side of each pita with oil. Place on a work surface, oiled side down, and evenly layer steak mixture over half of each pita, leaving a ½-inch (1 cm) border around the edges. Drizzle with tzatziki and sprinkle with feta. Fold pitas over filling, pressing gently to pack.

3. Place sandwiches in grill, close the top plate and cook until golden brown, 3 to 4 minutes. Serve immediately.

Patty Melt Panini

I love Swiss cheese on a patty melt, especially in this panini.

Serves 2

Tip

Set the top plate of the panini grill so that it just touches the sandwich; pressing too hard will cause the juices from the hamburger patty to run, creating soggy bread.

Variation

Add sliced jalapeño pepper or another hot green chile pepper for extra flavor and spice. To control the heat, remove the ribs and seeds.

Preheat panini grill to high

2 tsp	olive oil	10 mL
½	small red onion, thinly sliced	½
4	slices rye bread (½-inch/1 cm thick slices)	4
1 tbsp	butter, melted	15 mL
2	leftover cooked lean hamburger patties (½ inch/1 cm thick), reheated	2
2 oz	Swiss cheese, thinly sliced	60 g
Pinch	salt	Pinch
Pinch	freshly ground black pepper	Pinch

1. In a skillet, heat oil over medium–high heat. Add onion and sauté until softened, 7 to 9 minutes. Remove from heat and keep warm.

2. Brush one side of each bread slice with butter. Place two slices on a work surface, buttered side down, and place a beef patty on each slice. Evenly layer with cheese and onion. Sprinkle with salt and pepper. Cover with top halves, buttered side up, and press gently to pack.

3. Place sandwiches in grill, close the top plate and cook until golden brown, 3 to 4 minutes. Serve immediately.

Meatloaf Panini

I remember my mother's meatloaf fondly, but even though I'm an experienced chef, I cannot seem to replicate it. We never put her meatloaf in a sandwich, as there were never any leftovers.

Serves 2

Variations

Add another layer with leftover mashed potatoes and corn.

For a peppery taste, use arugula instead of romaine.

Preheat panini grill to high

4	slices sourdough bread (½-inch/1 cm thick slices)	4
1 tbsp	butter, melted	15 mL
1 tbsp	mayonnaise	15 mL
1 tbsp	ketchup	15 mL
2	slices leftover meatloaf (½-inch/1 cm thick slices), reheated	2
2 oz	provolone cheese, thinly sliced	60 g
4	thin slices tomato	4
2	romaine lettuce leaves	2

1. Brush one side of each bread slice with butter. Place on a work surface, buttered side down, and spread mayonnaise over bottom halves. Spread ketchup over top halves. On bottom halves, evenly layer with meatloaf, cheese, tomato and lettuce. Cover with top halves and press gently to pack.

2. Place sandwiches in grill, close the top plate so that it barely touches the sandwiches and cook until golden brown, 3 to 4 minutes. Serve immediately.

Pulled Pork Panini

I adore barbecue sandwiches from all areas of the South, especially those made with pulled pork, barbecue sauce and creamy coleslaw. Ciabatta rolls are sturdy and hold up to the juices in this sandwich. You will — as with so many of my panini recipes — need stacks of napkins.

Serves 2

Tips

Serve with the pickles of your choice — my favorite are bread and butter pickles.

Either creamy coleslaw or a vinegar-based coleslaw will work.

Preheat panini grill to high

2	ciabatta rolls, split	2
1 tbsp	butter, melted	15 mL
1 cup	leftover pulled pork	250 mL
1/3 cup	barbecue sauce (store-bought or see recipe, page 245)	75 mL
1/2 cup	well-drained coleslaw	125 mL

1. Place rolls, cut side down, on a work surface and brush crusts with butter. Turn rolls over and, on bottom halves, evenly layer with pulled pork. Drizzle with barbecue sauce and top with coleslaw. Cover with top halves and press gently to pack.

2. Place sandwiches in grill, close the top plate and cook until golden brown, 3 to 4 minutes. Serve immediately.

Pork Tenderloin and Brie Panini with Mango Chutney

Succulent pork tenderloin, creamy Brie and sweet and sassy mango chutney create a panini you cannot believe is made from leftovers.

Serves 2

Tip
Reheat the pork slices in the panini grill for 1 to 2 minutes before making the sandwich, if desired.

Variation
Substitute beef tenderloin for the pork.

Preheat panini grill to high

2	bolillo rolls (see tip, page 120), split	2
1 tbsp	olive oil	15 mL
2 tbsp	mango chutney	25 mL
6	thin slices leftover cooked pork tenderloin	6
2 oz	Brie cheese, rind removed, thinly sliced	60 g
1 tbsp	thinly sliced green onion	15 mL

1. Place rolls, cut side down, on a work surface and brush crusts with oil. Turn rolls over and spread chutney over bottom halves. Evenly layer with pork and cheese. Sprinkle with green onion. Cover with top halves and press gently to pack.

2. Place sandwiches in grill, close the top plate and cook until golden brown, 3 to 4 minutes. Serve immediately.

Ham, Pineapple and Sweet Potato Panini

Easter calls for a succulent ham roasted with pineapple slices, cloves and a honey glaze. Now you know what to do with the leftovers.

Serves 2

Tip

A thin layer of sweet potato works best in this recipe, giving the sandwich the right texture and density. You may need less than called for, depending on the size of the rolls.

Variation

Substitute dinner rolls for the ciabatta rolls.

Preheat panini grill to high

2	ciabatta rolls, split	2
1 tbsp	butter, melted	15 mL
½ cup	leftover mashed sweet potato, reheated	125 mL
2	slices leftover cooked ham (¼ to ½ inch/0.5 to 1 cm thick)	2
2	slices fresh pineapple (about ¼ inch/0.5 cm thick)	2

1. Place rolls, cut side down, on a work surface and brush crusts with butter. Turn rolls over and spread sweet potato over bottom halves. Evenly layer with ham and pineapple. Cover with top halves and press gently to pack.

2. Place sandwiches in grill, close the top plate and cook until golden brown, 3 to 4 minutes. Serve immediately.

Simply Kielbasa Panini

Kielbasa is good in so many recipes, and I love the flavor in this simple panini.

Serves 2

Variations

Add grilled onions or sauerkraut for incredible flavor.

Substitute your favorite cheese for the mozzarella.

Preheat panini grill to high

2	hoagie buns, split	2
1 tbsp	butter, melted	15 mL
1 tbsp	mayonnaise	15 mL
1 tbsp	spicy mustard	15 mL
4	slices leftover grilled kielbasa sausage (about ½ inch/1 cm thick)	2
½ cup	shredded mozzarella cheese	125 mL

1. Place buns, cut side down, on a work surface and brush crusts with butter. Turn buns over and spread mayonnaise over bottom halves. Spread mustard over top halves. On bottom halves, evenly layer with kielbasa and cheese. Cover with top halves and press gently to pack.

2. Place sandwiches in grill, close the top plate and cook until golden brown, 3 to 4 minutes. Serve immediately.

Monday Morning Quarterback Brat Panini

I am a Dallas Cowboy fan and have been my entire life. I am dating a Green Bay Packer fan, although the word "fan" does not truly describe his devotion. My idea of tailgating involves Brie cheese, sparkling wine and bruschetta, but TJ will settle for nothing less than a Midwest brat and ice-cold beer. Hence, I give you the Monday Morning Quarterback, made with bratwurst left over from Sunday's game-watching party.

Serves 2

Variations

There are many possible additions: grilled onions and peppers, chopped onions, pickled jalapeño peppers — the choices are endless.

Use kielbasa or Italian sausage in place of the bratwurst.

Try adding Jalapeño Mayonnaise (page 238) for extra heat.

Preheat panini grill to high

2	submarine rolls, split	2
1 tbsp	butter, melted	15 mL
1/4 cup	Chipotle Barbecue Sauce (see recipe, page 245)	50 mL
2	leftover cooked bratwurst sausages, split horizontally and reheated	2
1/2 cup	well-drained sauerkraut	125 mL

1. Place rolls, cut side down, on a work surface and brush crusts with butter. Turn rolls over and spread with barbecue sauce. On bottom halves, evenly layer with bratwurst and sauerkraut. Cover with top halves and press gently to pack.

2. Place sandwiches in grill, close the top plate and cook until golden brown, 3 to 4 minutes. Serve immediately.

My Favorite Chili Cheese Dog Melt

I love a good chili cheese dog — when I was growing up, it was one of my favorite comfort foods — but take my advice and eat these with a fork.

Serves 2

Tips

My little one loves hot dogs with ketchup, but I contend that the recipe is not the same if you do not use good old-fashioned mustard. You could add pickle relish or sweet relish on top of the onion.

I like to use whole wheat hot dog buns or hoagie buns.

Preheat panini grill to high

2	hot dog buns, split	2
1 tbsp	butter, melted	15 mL
1 tbsp	mustard	15 mL
2	leftover grilled all-beef hot dog wieners, halved lengthwise	2
½ cup	leftover chili	125 mL
½ cup	shredded Cheddar cheese	125 mL
¼ cup	diced white onion	50 mL

1. Place buns, cut side down, on a work surface and brush crusts with butter. Turn buns over and spread with mustard. Down the middle of each bun half, evenly layer with hot dogs, chili, cheese and onion.

2. Place sandwiches in grill, lower the top plate to within ½ inch (1 cm) of the filling and hold until cheese is melted, 1 to 2 minutes. Serve immediately, open-faced.

Panini
Just for Kids

Jammin' Pancake Panini

Kids love to cook, so why not involve them in the preparation? Have kids help smear on the cream cheese and jam and layer the sliced banana.

Serves 2

Tip

Freshly squeezed orange juice on the side makes this the perfect morning breakfast for the kids.

Variations

Try adding link or breakfast sausage for more protein.

This is great with diced fresh strawberries, either in the panini or on the side.

Preheat panini grill to high
Cookie cutter of desired shape

4	pancakes (each about 4 to 5 inches/ 10 to 12.5 cm in diameter)	4
1 tbsp	butter, melted	15 mL
2 tbsp	cream cheese, softened	25 mL
2 tbsp	strawberry jam	25 mL
1	banana, sliced	1
2 tbsp	liquid honey	25 mL

1. Brush one side of each pancake with butter. Place on a work surface, buttered side down, and spread cream cheese over bottom halves. Spread jam over top halves. On bottom halves, evenly layer with banana and drizzle with honey. Cover with top halves and press gently to pack. Using the cookie cutter, cut into desired shape.

2. Place sandwiches in grill, close the top plate and cook until lightly toasted and grill-marked, 1 to 2 minutes. Serve immediately.

Green Eggs and Ham Panini

Serve this recipe in honor of the Dr. Seuss classic Green Eggs and Ham. *Both kids and adults will enjoy this recipe.*

Serves 2

Tip
This sandwich is not just for kids; I love it with a mimosa and a Dr. Seuss story!

Variation
Most kids love cheese, so add the cheese of your choice for dairy.

Preheat panini grill to high

1 tsp	butter	5 mL
½ cup	diced ham	125 mL
½ cup	thinly sliced baby spinach	125 mL
1 tbsp	chopped green onion	15 mL
2	eggs, beaten	2
Pinch	salt	Pinch
Pinch	freshly ground pepper	Pinch
2	English muffins, split	2
1 tbsp	butter, melted	15 mL
1 tbsp	freshly grated Parmesan cheese	15 mL

1. In a nonstick skillet, melt 1 tsp (5 mL) butter over medium-high heat. Add ham and sauté for 1 minute. Add spinach and green onion; sauté for 1 minute. Add eggs, salt and pepper; scramble until eggs are desired consistency.

2. Place muffins, cut side down on a work surface, and brush crusts with melted butter. Turn muffins over and divide egg mixture evenly between bottom halves. Sprinkle with cheese. Cover with top halves and press gently to pack.

3. Place sandwiches in grill, close the top plate and cook until golden brown, 3 to 4 minutes. Serve immediately.

Cinnamon Raisin Apple Panini

I have made this recipe on television, with rave reviews from parents. This recipe is great for hands-on cooking with kids.

Serves 2

Tips

Kids can help prepare this healthy, fun treat at home or in the classroom.

Use your favorite apple variety — McIntosh and Granny Smith work particularly well.

Preheat panini grill to high

4	slices cinnamon raisin bread (½-inch/1 cm thick slices)	4
1 tbsp	butter, melted	15 mL
2 oz	Cheddar cheese, thinly sliced	60 g
1	small apple, thinly sliced	1

1. Brush one side of each bread slice with butter. Place two slices on a work surface, buttered side down, and evenly layer with cheese and apple. Cover with top halves, buttered side up, and press gently to pack.

2. Place sandwiches in grill, close the top plate and cook until golden brown, 3 to 4 minutes. Serve immediately.

Ants in a Panini

No, this sandwich isn't made with real ants — it's just a catchy title for panini packed with raisins and sweetened cream cheese, melted in challah bread.

Serves 2

Tips

For variety, use golden raisins or substitute dried cranberries.

Try this recipe with strawberry-flavored cream cheese.

Preheat panini grill to high

2 tsp	granulated sugar	10 mL
¼ tsp	ground cinnamon, divided	1 mL
¼ cup	cream cheese, softened	50 mL
1 tbsp	confectioner's (icing) sugar	15 mL
Dash	vanilla extract	Dash
4	slices challah bread (½-inch/1 cm thick slices)	4
1 tbsp	butter, melted	15 mL
2 tbsp	raisins	25 mL

1. In a bowl, combine confectioner's sugar and a pinch of cinnamon; set aside.

2. In another bowl, combine cream cheese, sugar, the remaining cinnamon and vanilla.

3. Brush one side of each bread slice with butter and sprinkle with cinnamon-sugar, pressing so it sticks. Place two slices on a work surface, buttered side down, and spread with cream cheese mixture. Sprinkle with raisins. Cover with top halves, buttered side up, and press gently to pack.

4. Place sandwiches in grill, close the top plate and cook until golden brown, 3 to 4 minutes. Serve immediately.

PB&J and Banana Panini

This recipe brings peanut butter to new heights. My daughter loves this all-American sandwich to begin with, but when it's toasted in the panini maker, she is in heaven! I often leave the banana off and use creamy peanut butter with a variety of jelly flavors.

Serves 2

Tip
If your bananas are too ripe, the slices will slide out. The solution? Mash them.

Variation
Use challah bread or cinnamon raisin bread instead of wheat bread.

Preheat panini grill to high

4	slices wheat bread (1-inch/2.5 cm thick slices)	4
1 tbsp	butter, softened	15 mL
1/4 cup	crunchy peanut butter	50 mL
2 tbsp	strawberry preserves or jam	25 mL
1	banana, sliced	1

1. Spread one side of each bread slice with butter. Place on a work surface, buttered side down, and spread with peanut butter. On bottom halves, evenly spread with preserves and layer with banana. Cover with top halves and press gently to pack.

2. Place sandwiches in grill, close the top plate and cook until golden brown, 3 to 4 minutes. Serve immediately.

Grilled Cheese Panini Stars

Kids of all ages love grilled cheese because it's a feel-good comfort food — especially when cut into stars. American cheese is great on its own, but the combination of mozzarella and American cheese is truly a winner.

Serves 2

Tip

This recipe is great for parties and sleepovers, and it's the perfect treat for your little ones when they win the soccer tournament, bring home a good report card or take out the recycle bin without being asked.

Preheat panini grill to high
Star-shaped cookie cutter

4	slices wheat bread ($\frac{1}{2}$-inch/1 cm thick slices)	4
2 oz	white American cheese, thinly sliced	60 g
2 oz	mozzarella cheese, thinly sliced	60 g
	Olive oil spray	

1. Using cookie cutter, cut bread and cheese into stars.

2. Lightly spray one side of each bread slice with olive oil. Place on a work surface, oiled side down, and evenly layer American cheese and mozzarella on bottom halves. Cover with top halves and press gently to pack.

3. Place sandwiches in grill, close the top plate and cook until golden brown, 3 to 4 minutes. Serve immediately.

Plain Ole Chicken and Cheese Panini

Yes, this is a plain combination, but guess what? They will eat it! It is so hard to find recipes kids will eat, so stick with the basics and turn them into a panini.

Serves 2

Tip

Some kids do not like mayonnaise, mustard or anything of the like; simply omit anything your child doesn't like.

Variation

Substitute ham, turkey or roast beef for the chicken.

Preheat panini grill to high

2	slices French bread (½-inch/1 cm thick slices)	2
1 tbsp	butter, melted	15 mL
1 tbsp	honey mustard	15 mL
1 tbsp	mayonnaise	15 mL
2 oz	deli roasted chicken breast, thinly sliced	60 g
2 oz	white American cheese, thinly sliced	60 g

1. Brush one side of each bread slice with butter. Place on a work surface, buttered side down, and spread honey mustard over bottom halves. Spread mayonnaise over top halves. On bottom halves, evenly layer with chicken and cheese. Cover with top halves and press gently to pack.

2. Place sandwiches in grill, close the top plate and cook until golden brown, 3 to 4 minutes. Serve immediately.

Dinner Roll Turkey and Ham Panini

This panini recipe is perfect for little hands and is great with leftover dinner rolls. I keep cooked dinner rolls in the freezer, then thaw them to room temperature to serve with soup or a snack.

Serves 2

Tip

I have discovered that most children love dinner rolls. Feel free to substitute your child's favorite ingredients. One little friend of mine enjoys fish sticks as a panini filling — now that is a specialty sandwich!

Preheat panini grill to high

2	dinner rolls, split	2
2 tsp	butter, melted	10 mL
2 oz	deli ham, thinly sliced	60 g
2 oz	deli turkey breast, thinly sliced	60 g
2 oz	white Cheddar cheese, thinly sliced	60 g

1. Place rolls, cut side down, on a work surface and brush crusts with butter. Turn rolls over and, on bottom halves, evenly layer with ham, turkey and cheese. Cover with top halves and press gently to pack.

2. Place sandwiches in grill, close the top plate and cook until golden brown, 3 to 4 minutes. Serve immediately.

Crazy Crunch Panini

My little friend Emmy loves to put crushed chips on sandwiches, which proves my theory: kids love crunch! For a bit of family fun, have the kids crush the chips. Tortilla chips will give more crunch than potato chips, especially after the sandwiches are grilled.

Serves 2

Tip
To lighten up this recipe, use baked chips instead of fried.

Preheat panini grill to high

4	slices wheat bread (½-inch/1 cm thick slices)	4
1 tbsp	butter, melted	15 mL
2 oz	white American cheese, thinly sliced	60 g
1 oz	deli baked ham, thinly sliced	30 g
1 oz	deli smoked turkey breast, thinly sliced	30 g
¼ cup	crushed potato or tortilla chips	50 mL

1. Brush one side of each bread slice with butter. Place two slices on a work surface, buttered side down, and evenly layer with cheese, ham, turkey and crushed chips. Cover with top halves, buttered side up, and press gently to pack.

2. Place sandwiches in grill, close the top plate and cook until golden brown, 3 to 4 minutes. Serve immediately.

Pineapple Ham Panini

Fresh pineapple is so good, but for convenience, canned will do the trick.

Serves 2

Variations

Spread the bread with flavored cream cheese before adding the fillings. Our favorite flavors are strawberry and vanilla.

Substitute white American cheese for the Cheddar, or use both.

Preheat panini grill to high

4	slices multigrain bread (½-inch/1 cm thick slices)	4
1 tbsp	butter, melted	15 mL
2 oz	Cheddar cheese, thinly sliced	60 g
2 oz	deli ham, thinly sliced	60 g
2	slices fresh pineapple (about ¼ inch/0.5 cm thick)	2

1. Brush one side of each bread slice with butter. Place two slices on a work surface, buttered side down, and evenly layer with cheese, ham and pineapple. Cover with top halves, buttered side up, and press gently to pack.

2. Place sandwiches in grill, close the top plate and cook until golden brown, 3 to 4 minutes. Serve immediately.

Pineapple Pizza Panini

Let's face it: kids love pizza. There are numerous recipes in this book that include pizza ingredients, but this one has all the flavors that kids typically love. My tween friend Derek never knew pineapple was so good in a sandwich; now he wants it on everything.

Serves 2

Tips

Lighten up this recipe by using part-skim mozzarella.

For lots of color, use a variety of bell peppers: green, red, yellow, orange or purple.

Variation

Use ciabatta rolls instead of tortillas and make sandwiches rather than wraps.

Preheat panini grill to high

2	6-inch (15 cm) flour tortillas	2
1 tbsp	butter, melted	15 mL
2 tbsp	pizza sauce	25 mL
2 oz	deli smoked ham, thinly sliced	60 g
1/4 cup	chopped seeded tomato	50 mL
1/4 cup	chopped bell pepper (any color)	50 mL
1/4 cup	drained canned pineapple tidbits	50 mL
1/2 cup	shredded mozzarella cheese	125 mL

1. Brush one side of each tortilla with butter. Place on a work surface, buttered side down, and spread with pizza sauce. Down the center of each tortilla, evenly layer ham, tomato, bell pepper, pineapple and cheese, leaving a 1/2-inch (1 cm) border at each end. Fold both sides over center, overlapping sides, and press gently to pack.

2. Place sandwiches in grill, close the top plate, and cook until golden brown, 3 to 4 minutes. Serve immediately.

Pressed Pizza Panini

The fillings in this recipe are just suggestions — every kid has different preferences when it comes to pizza toppings. Use your imagination to create your very own pizza panini, and you will have a true winner.

Serves 2

Tip

Lighten up this recipe by using part-skim mozzarella and low-fat mayonnaise.

Variations

For a change of pace, substitute Canadian bacon or cooked ground beef for the pepperoni. Look for precooked crumbled lean ground beef to keep kitchen prep work simple.

Sneak in baby spinach leaves for iron.

Preheat panini grill to high

2 tbsp	mayonnaise	25 mL
½ tsp	dried Italian seasoning	2 mL
4	slices Italian bread (½-inch/1 cm thick slices)	4
1 tbsp	butter, melted	15 mL
3 oz	turkey pepperoni, thinly sliced	90 g
½ cup	shredded mozzarella cheese	125 mL
1	plum (Roma) tomato, thinly sliced	1

1. In a bowl, combine mayonnaise and Italian seasoning.

2. Brush one side of each bread slice with butter. Place on a work surface, buttered side down, and spread with mayonnaise mixture. On bottom halves, evenly layer with pepperoni, cheese and tomato. Cover with top halves and press gently to pack.

3. Place sandwiches in grill, close the top plate and cook until golden brown, 3 to 4 minutes. Serve immediately.

Open-Face Hawaiian Melt

My daughter, Kennedy, loves this flavor combination, so I decided to put it in a panini, and voila! What a kid pleaser! The best part is, she likes to help me make this panini, which gives us time together and builds her confidence in the kitchen.

Serves 2

Tips

For family time, have kids help assemble the sandwiches. They will be so pleased with the outcome.

Use store-bought tomato sauce, marinara sauce or pizza sauce for convenience.

Variation

Hot dog buns are certainly a kid favorite, but another alternative is ciabatta rolls. Slice off the domed top before splitting the rolls in half horizontally. This makes for a much flatter panini, with a texture little ones will love.

Preheat panini grill to high

2	hot dog buns, split	2
2 tbsp	butter, melted	25 mL
1/4 cup	tomato sauce	50 mL
1/4 cup	shredded mozzarella cheese	50 mL
1/4 cup	drained canned pineapple tidbits	50 mL
4	slices Canadian bacon, cut into thin strips	4

1. Open hot dog buns flat and brush butter on all sides. Place in grill, close the top plate and cook until lightly toasted, 1 to 2 minutes. Transfer from grill to a work surface and spread tomato sauce on cut sides. Evenly layer with cheese, pineapple and bacon.

2. Return assembled sandwiches to the grill, lower the top plate to within 1/2 inch (1 cm) of the filling and hold until cheese is melted, 1 to 2 minutes. Serve immediately, open-faced.

Fiesta Panini

This is a colorful recipe that's perfect for getting kids to eat their veggies. Use low-fat cream cheese or flavored cream cheese for variety. My little friend Griffin loves the addition of shredded chicken breast and guacamole to this recipe.

Serves 2

Tips

Drain and rinse canned black beans under cool running water to remove the starchy film.

You know your kids and what they will eat. You can sneak in veggies from time to time, but use ones they like. Shredded carrots, for example, are a great addition to this recipe.

Preheat panini grill to high

¼ cup	drained rinsed canned black beans	50 mL
¼ cup	frozen corn kernels, thawed	50 mL
¼ cup	thinly sliced green bell pepper	50 mL
¼ cup	cream cheese, softened	50 mL
1 tbsp	mild salsa	15 mL
2	6-inch (15 cm) flour tortillas	2
1 tbsp	butter, melted	15 mL
4	slices bacon, diced and cooked crisp	4
½ cup	shredded Colby-Jack or Monterey Jack cheese	125 mL

1. In a bowl, combine beans, corn and green pepper; set aside.

2. In another bowl, combine cream cheese and salsa.

3. Brush one side of each tortilla with butter. Place on a work surface, buttered side down, and spread with cream cheese mixture. Evenly layer bean mixture, bacon and cheese over half of each tortilla, leaving a ½-inch (1 cm) border around the edges. Fold tortillas over filling, pressing gently to pack.

4. Place sandwiches in grill, close the top plate and cook until golden brown, 3 to 4 minutes. Serve immediately.

Cheesy Beanie Panini

Bean burritos are wonderful and even better pressed in a panini. Give the kids topping options to personalize their Cheesy Beanie Panini.

Serves 2

Tips

If your family likes a bit of spice, use pinto beans canned with jalapeños.

Mashed black beans also work well in this recipe.

Preheat panini grill to high

½ cup	drained rinsed canned pinto beans	125 mL
2	6-inch (15 cm) flour tortillas	2
1 tbsp	butter, melted	15 mL
½ cup	shredded Monterey Jack cheese	125 mL
	Sour cream, ranch dressing, shredded lettuce, chopped tomatoes and salsa	

1. With the back of a fork, mash beans to a chunky consistency.

2. Brush one side of each tortilla with butter. Place on a work surface, buttered side down, and spread with mashed beans. Sprinkle cheese over half of each tortilla, leaving a ½-inch (1 cm) border around the edges. Fold tortillas over filling, pressing gently to pack.

3. Place sandwiches in grill, close the top plate and cook until golden brown, 3 to 4 minutes. Serve immediately, and top with sour cream, ranch dressing, lettuce, tomatoes and salsa, as desired.

Chocolate, Peanut Butter and Banana Panini

You have to have chocolate in the kids chapter, and here it is: peanut butter and banana with chocolate chips. Leave off the banana if it gets in the way of the chocolate — oh, go ahead and splurge: double up on the chocolate!

Serves 2

Variations

Add a sprinkle of granola cereal for crunch and fiber.

Blueberries and sliced strawberries make great additions.

Stuff a few mini marshmallows into this panini for gooey goodness.

Preheat panini grill to high

4	slices challah bread (½-inch/1 cm thick slices)	4
1 tbsp	butter, melted	15 mL
¼ cup	crunchy peanut butter	50 mL
1	small banana, sliced	1
2 tbsp	semisweet chocolate chips	25 mL

1. Brush one side of each bread slice with butter. Place two slices on a work surface, buttered side down, and spread with peanut butter. Evenly layer with banana and sprinkle with chocolate chips. Cover with top halves, buttered side up, and press to pack.

2. Place sandwiches in grill, close the top plate and cook until golden brown, 3 to 4 minutes. Serve immediately.

Banana Split Panini

This recipe is a favorite for kids, including adult kids who love banana splits. It's quite messy, but the exceptional flavor makes it well worth the cleanup.

Serves 2

Variation

Add toasted chopped nuts for more flavor and crunch.

Preheat panini grill to high

4	slices honey wheat bread (½-inch/1 cm thick slices)	4
1 tbsp	butter, melted	15 mL
2 tbsp	creamy peanut butter	25 mL
1	banana, sliced	1
½ cup	thinly sliced strawberries	125 mL
1 tbsp	liquid honey	15 mL
1 tbsp	chocolate syrup	15 mL
2 tbsp	whipped cream	25 mL
2	maraschino cherries (with stems)	2

1. Brush one side of each bread slice with butter. Place two slices on a work surface, buttered side down, and spread with peanut butter. Evenly layer with banana and strawberries. Drizzle with honey and chocolate syrup. Cover with top halves, buttered side up, and press gently to pack.

2. Place sandwiches in grill, close the top plate and cook until golden brown, 3 to 4 minutes. Serve immediately, topped with whipped cream and cherries.

Desserts

Apple Caramel Panini

When this panini comes off the grill, you will love the ooey-gooey caramel goodness, which reminds me of caramel-dipped apples from Halloween!

Serves 2

Tip

Use a cookie cutter to cut the bread into fun shapes. Let the kids help and turn it into a family activity.

Variation

Add nuts to the filling for even more flavor.

Preheat panini grill to high

1 tsp	granulated sugar	5 mL
¼ tsp	ground cinnamon	1 mL
4	slices challah bread (½-inch/1 cm thick slices)	4
1 tbsp	butter, melted	15 mL
¼ cup	caramel sauce	50 mL
1	small Granny Smith apple, peeled and very thinly sliced	1

1. In a small bowl, combine sugar and cinnamon; set aside.

2. Brush one side of each bread slice with butter. Place on a work surface, buttered side down, and drizzle with caramel sauce. On bottom halves, evenly arrange apple slices and sprinkle with sugar mixture. Cover with top halves and press gently to pack.

3. Place sandwiches in grill, close the top plate and cook until golden brown, 3 to 4 minutes. Serve immediately.

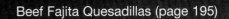
Beef Fajita Quesadillas (page 195)

Jammin' Pancake Panini (page 206)

Pineapple Ham Panini (page 215)

Banana Split Panini (page 222)

Black Bean and Corn Salsa (page 248)
and Perfect Guacamole (page 249)

Cranberry Sauce (page 244)

Simple Strawberry Shortcakes (page 228)

Mixed Berry and Mascarpone Panini with
Toasted Almonds (page 227)

Honeyed Cream Cheese and Apple Panini

Slightly sweetened cream cheese is terrific in this apple panini. I choose McIntosh apples, as they cook so well, but you can certainly use the apple of your choice. Granny Smith apples, for example, have the perfect amount of tartness.

Serves 2

Tips

Cinnamon bread is a good choice if you cannot find challah.

The cream cheese mixture is a tasty treat when smeared on homemade biscuits, toast or crackers and topped with fruit jam or preserves.

Spray your measuring spoon with nonstick cooking spray before measuring the honey — it will slide right off.

Preheat panini grill to high

¼ cup	cream cheese, softened	50 mL
4 tsp	liquid honey, divided	20 mL
¼ tsp	vanilla extract	1 mL
4	slices challah bread (½-inch/1 cm thick slices)	4
1 tbsp	butter, melted	15 mL
1	McIntosh apple, thinly sliced	1
Pinch	ground cinnamon	Pinch
Pinch	ground nutmeg	Pinch
½ cup	raspberries, blueberries or sliced strawberries	125 mL

1. In a small bowl, combine cream cheese, 1 tsp (5 mL) of the honey and vanilla; set aside.

2. Brush one side of each bread slice with butter. Place on a work surface, buttered side down, and spread with cream cheese mixture. On bottom halves, evenly arrange apple slices and sprinkle with cinnamon and nutmeg. Cover with top halves and press gently to pack.

3. Place sandwiches in grill, close the top plate and cook until golden brown, 3 to 4 minutes. Serve immediately, drizzled with the remaining honey and sprinkled with berries.

Peach Blueberry Dessert

This lovely dessert will get rave reviews both for its beautiful presentation and for its great flavor combination.

Serves 2

Tips

White chocolate ice cream is also wonderful with this.

Freshly whipped cream is so good when you add amaretto to it; dollop it on top of the ice cream, then sprinkle with the almonds.

Preheat panini grill to high

2	peaches, peeled and sliced	2
½ cup	blueberries	125 mL
3 tbsp	granulated sugar	45 mL
2 tsp	freshly squeezed lemon juice	10 mL
2	slices pound cake (½-inch/1 cm thick slices)	2
1 tbsp	butter, melted	15 mL
2	small scoops vanilla ice cream	2
2 tbsp	amaretto or other almond-flavored liqueur	25 mL
2 tbsp	chopped almonds, toasted (see tip, page 227)	25 mL

1. In a bowl, combine peaches, blueberries, sugar and lemon juice; let stand, stirring occasionally, until sugar is dissolved and fruit is juicy, about 10 minutes.

2. Place cake on a work surface and brush both sides with butter. Place in grill, close the top plate and cook until lightly toasted and grill-marked, 2 to 3 minutes.

3. Transfer cake to small dessert plates. Spoon peach mixture over cake and top with ice cream. Drizzle with amaretto and sprinkle with almonds. Serve immediately.

Mixed Berry and Mascarpone Panini with Toasted Almonds

In this amazing recipe, buttery-rich mascarpone is the star, with supporting roles played by toasted almonds and tart berries laced with Kirsch.

Serves 2

Tips

Serve with a cold glass of brut Champagne.

To toast nuts, spread them evenly on a baking sheet and toast in a 350°F (180°C) oven until fragrant and light brown, 5 to 10 minutes.

Preheat panini grill to high

¼ cup	raspberries	50 mL
¼ cup	sliced strawberries	50 mL
¼ cup	blueberries	50 mL
1 tsp	granulated sugar	5 mL
1 tsp	Kirsch or other cherry-flavored liqueur	5 mL
4	slices brioche (½-inch/1 cm thick slices)	4
1 tbsp	butter, melted	15 mL
¼ cup	mascarpone cheese, softened	50 mL
2 tbsp	slivered almonds, toasted (see tip, at left)	25 mL
	Confectioner's (icing) sugar	
	Whipped cream	

1. In a bowl, combine raspberries, strawberries, blueberries, sugar and Kirsch; let stand, stirring occasionally, until sugar is dissolved and berries are juicy, about 30 minutes. Drain off excess liquid.

2. Brush one side of each bread slice with butter. Place on a work surface, buttered side down, spread with cheese and sprinkle with almonds. On bottom halves, evenly arrange berry mixture. Cover with top halves and press gently to pack.

3. Place sandwiches in grill, close the top plate and cook until golden brown, 3 to 4 minutes. Serve immediately, sprinkled with confectioner's sugar and topped with whipped cream.

Simple Strawberry Shortcakes

I always loved it when my mom made strawberry shortcake — what a treat! I decided to put my own twist on it by making it into a panini and adding a bit of good-quality balsamic vinegar for an unexpected flavor.

Serves 2

Tips

There is nothing better than fresh strawberries in season, but if you need to, use thawed frozen strawberries and add a bit of lemon juice for freshness.

This is a great summertime dessert, especially for the Fourth of July or Canada Day. For a red, white and blue theme, add fresh blueberries or blackberries to the mix.

If you have butter-flavored cooking spray, it works much better in this recipe than melted butter.

Variation

For real Southern flair, use leftover biscuits instead of the cake.

Preheat panini grill to high

2 cups	sliced strawberries	500 mL
3 tbsp	granulated sugar	45 mL
¼ tsp	balsamic vinegar	1 mL
4	slices angel food cake or pound cake (½-inch/1 cm thick slices)	4
	Butter-flavored cooking spray or 1 tbsp (15 mL) butter, melted	
⅓ cup	whipped cream	75 mL
2	sprigs fresh mint	2

1. In a bowl, combine strawberries, sugar and vinegar; let stand, stirring occasionally, until sugar is dissolved and strawberries are juicy, about 30 minutes.

2. Place cake on a work surface and spray or brush both sides with butter. Place in grill, close the top plate and cook until lightly toasted and grill-marked, 2 to 3 minutes.

3. Place one cake slice on each of two dessert plates. Spread each with 1 tbsp (15 mL) whipped cream. Evenly layer strawberry mixture over whipped cream. Dollop each with another 1 tbsp (15 mL) whipped cream. Cover with the remaining cake slices and top with the remaining whipped cream and mint sprigs. Serve immediately.

Honey and Brie Panini

One day, my dear friend Susan was craving a panini, but had nothing on hand except for bread and Brie. Not to be discouraged, she added a bit of flair with honey, and voila: a simple but delicious masterpiece!

Serves 2

Tips

I've tried this recipe with numerous bread selections, and my favorite was sourdough. I found cinnamon bread too sweet, and wheat bread just didn't have enough oomph. You decide.

Fresh or dried fruit is great inside this panini as well.

Preheat panini grill to high

4	slices sourdough bread (½-inch/1 cm thick slices)	4
1 tbsp	butter, melted	15 mL
¼ cup	liquid honey	50 mL
2 oz	Brie cheese, rind removed, thinly sliced	60 g
	Chopped fresh fruit	

1. Brush one side of each bread slice with butter. Place on a work surface, buttered side down, and drizzle with honey. On bottom halves, evenly arrange Brie. Cover with top halves and press gently to pack.

2. Place sandwiches in grill, close the top plate and cook until golden brown, 3 to 4 minutes. Serve immediately, drizzled with honey and sprinkled with fresh fruit.

S'mores Panini

I have to admit, camping is not my thing — but s'mores definitely are! I developed this recipe so I could have my s'mores by the panini maker instead of by the fire.

Serves 2

Tips

You can certainly use large marshmallows, white or colored, in place of the marshmallow cream.

I used a milk chocolate bar, but for a more intense flavor, try dark chocolate.

Preheat panini grill to high

4	slices challah bread (½-inch/1 cm thick slices)	4
1 tbsp	butter, melted	15 mL
½ cup	marshmallow cream (fluff)	125 mL
2	graham crackers, broken in half	2
1	chocolate bar (1.55 oz/44 g), broken in half	1

1. Brush one side of each bread slice with butter. Place on a work surface, buttered side down, and spread with marshmallow cream. On bottom halves, evenly layer with graham crackers and chocolate. Cover with top halves and press gently to pack.

2. Place sandwiches in grill, close the top plate and cook until golden brown, 3 to 4 minutes. Serve immediately.

Triple-Chocolate Panini

Can't decide which chocolate to use? Use them all! Chocolate lovers will adore this recipe.

Serves 2

Tips

Go ahead and indulge yourself! Remember, moderation in the diet is key, but that doesn't mean you don't deserve the occasional treat.

Serve with fresh berries dusted with confectioner's (icing) sugar.

Preheat panini grill to high

½ oz	milk chocolate, chopped	15 g
½ oz	bittersweet chocolate, chopped	15 g
4	slices sourdough bread (½-inch/1 cm thick slices)	4
1 tbsp	butter, melted	15 mL
½ oz	semisweet chocolate, chopped	15 g

1. In a small bowl, combine milk chocolate and bittersweet chocolate; set aside.

2. Brush one side of each bread slice with butter. Place two slices on a work surface, buttered side down, and sprinkle with chocolate mixture, leaving a ¼-inch (0.5 cm) border around the edges. Cover with top halves, buttered side up, and press gently to pack.

3. Place sandwiches in grill, close the top plate and cook until golden brown, 3 to 4 minutes.

4. Meanwhile, place semisweet chocolate in a microwave-safe bowl sprayed with cooking spray. Microwave on High for 30-second intervals, removing to stir every 30 seconds, until almost melted. Stir until melted and smooth.

5. Remove sandwiches from grill and slice in half. Serve immediately, drizzled with melted chocolate.

Chocolate, Hazelnut and Strawberry Panini

This recipe is for anyone with a sweet tooth! It's especially nice after a romantic dinner for two, and makes an easy snack too.

Serves 2

Tips

Try topping these sandwiches with whipped cream or vanilla ice cream.

Chocolate-hazelnut spread can be found near the peanut butter at your grocery store.

Variation

Use pound cake or angel food cake in place of the challah bread.

Preheat panini grill to high

4	slices challah bread (½-inch/1 cm thick slices)	4
2 tsp	butter, melted	10 mL
¼ cup	chocolate-hazelnut spread (such as Nutella)	50 mL
½ cup	sliced strawberries	125 mL

1. Brush one side of each bread slice with butter. Place on a work surface, buttered side down, and spread with chocolate-hazelnut spread. On bottom halves, evenly arrange strawberries. Cover with top halves and press to pack.

2. Place sandwiches in grill, close the top plate and cook until golden brown, 3 to 4 minutes. Serve immediately.

Condiments

Basic Vinaigrette

This recipe is so simple, yet so good drizzled on salads, sandwiches or steamed vegetables.

Makes about ¾ cup (175 mL)

Tip

Store in an airtight container in the refrigerator for up to 1 week. Shake well before using.

Variation

Add about 2 tbsp (25 mL) minced fresh herbs to create herbed variations.

¼ cup	rice vinegar, white wine vinegar or freshly squeezed lemon juice	50 mL
½ tsp	salt	2 mL
¼ tsp	freshly ground black pepper	1 mL
½ cup	olive oil	125 mL

1. In a blender or food processor fitted with a metal blade, combine vinegar, salt and pepper. With the motor running, through the hole in the top or the feed tube, gradually add oil in a slow, steady stream; process until combined.

Tahini Dressing

This recipe is perfect as a spread for panini, as a dressing for salads or as a dip for crisp pita chips.

Makes about ½ cup (125 mL)

Tips

Store in an airtight container in the refrigerator for up to 1 week.

Tahini, a paste made of ground sesame seeds, is a key ingredient in Middle Eastern cuisine and is often used in hummus and salad dressings.

2	cloves garlic	2
⅓ cup	tahini	75 mL
⅓ cup	water	75 mL
¼ cup	freshly squeezed lemon juice	50 mL
1 tsp	soy sauce	5 mL
½ tsp	salt	2 mL
¼ tsp	paprika	1 mL
Pinch	freshly ground black pepper	Pinch
1 tbsp	chopped fresh parsley	15 mL

1. In a food processor, pulse garlic, tahini, water, lemon juice, soy sauce, salt, paprika and pepper until blended. Add parsley and pulse until finely chopped.

Russian Dressing

Spread or drizzle this dressing on panini ingredients before packing the sandwiches. It also makes a great salad dressing for your favorite green or garden salad.

Makes about ¾ cup (175 mL)

Tip
Store in an airtight container in the refrigerator for up to 3 days. Shake well before using.

Variation
For a thicker, creamier version, whisk in 1 tbsp (15 mL) mayonnaise.

⅓ cup	ketchup	75 mL
3 tbsp	grated onion	45 mL
2 tbsp	liquid honey	25 mL
2 tbsp	freshly squeezed lemon juice	25 mL
1 tsp	Worcestershire sauce	5 mL
½ tsp	salt	2 mL
¼ tsp	paprika	1 mL
3 tbsp	olive oil	45 mL

1. In a bowl, combine ketchup, onion, honey, lemon juice, Worcestershire sauce, salt and paprika. Quickly whisk in oil. Cover and refrigerate until chilled, about 20 minutes.

Thousand Island Dressing

Thousand Island dressing was a staple when I was growing up. I love this fresh version.

Makes about 1½ cups (375 mL)

Tips
Store in an airtight container in the refrigerator for up to 1 week. Shake well before using.

Drizzle this dressing on a lettuce wedge topped with chopped tomatoes, crumbled crispy bacon and freshly ground black pepper.

1 cup	mayonnaise	250 mL
2 tbsp	ketchup	25 mL
2 tsp	granulated sugar	10 mL
1 tsp	salt	5 mL
½ tsp	freshly ground black pepper	2 mL
2 tsp	freshly squeezed lemon juice	10 mL
1 tsp	Dijon mustard	5 mL
2 tbsp	olive oil	25 mL
1 tbsp	sweet relish	15 mL
¼ cup	grated onion	50 mL

1. In a bowl, combine mayonnaise, ketchup, sugar, salt, pepper, lemon juice and mustard. Quickly whisk in olive oil. Gently stir in relish and onion. Cover and refrigerate until chilled, about 20 minutes.

Basil Mayonnaise

Basil mayonnaise has such a fresh flavor, especially when you use basil from your own herb garden. You will love this fragrant spread on panini.

Makes about 1 cup (250 mL)

Tip

Store in an airtight container in the refrigerator for up to 1 week.

1 cup	mayonnaise	250 mL
¼ cup	loosely packed fresh basil leaves	50 mL
1 tsp	grated lemon zest	5 mL
1 tbsp	freshly squeezed lemon juice	15 mL
¼ tsp	garlic powder	1 mL

1. In a food processor, pulse mayonnaise, basil, lemon zest, lemon juice and garlic powder until smooth. Cover and refrigerate until chilled, about 20 minutes.

Sun-Dried Tomato Mayonnaise

This flavored mayonnaise enlivens poultry, beef, pork and vegetarian panini recipes.

Makes about 1¼ cups (300 mL)

Tips

Store in an airtight container in the refrigerator for up to 1 week. Stir before using.

Toss a couple of tablespoonfuls (25 mL) of this mayonnaise with hot pasta, top with freshly shaved Parmesan cheese, and voila — a perfectly simple but delicious meal.

¼ cup	drained oil-packed sun-dried tomatoes	50 mL
1 tbsp	freshly squeezed lemon juice	15 mL
¼ tsp	dried rosemary	1 mL
¼ tsp	dried basil	1 mL
1 cup	mayonnaise	250 mL

1. In a food processor, pulse tomatoes, lemon juice, rosemary and basil until tomatoes are finely chopped. Add mayonnaise and pulse until combined. Cover and refrigerate until chilled, about 20 minutes.

Blue Cheese Mayonnaise

This flavored mayonnaise is a wonderful addition to panini, especially beef panini. The blue cheese gives an extra bite to almost any ingredient lineup.

**Makes about
¾ cup (175 mL)**

Tips

Store in an airtight container in the refrigerator for up to 1 week.

Be careful not to overmix after adding the blue cheese, or you will end up with a mayonnaise that has a blue tint. Not very appetizing.

½ cup	mayonnaise	125 mL
¼ cup	plain yogurt	50 mL
2 tsp	freshly squeezed lemon juice	10 mL
2 oz	blue cheese, crumbled	60 g
¼ tsp	salt (or to taste)	1 mL

1. In a bowl, combine mayonnaise, yogurt and lemon juice. Carefully fold in blue cheese. Season to taste with salt. Cover and refrigerate until chilled, about 20 minutes.

Chipotle Mayonnaise

I love the kick this mayonnaise adds to sandwiches. If you want even more heat, just add more chipotle peppers.

**Makes about
1 cup (250 mL)**

Tips

Store in an airtight container in the refrigerator for up to 1 week.

I make a spicy coleslaw using shredded cabbage and carrots, chopped green onions and chipotle mayonnaise. It's a perfect side dish or stuffing for panini recipes.

1 cup	mayonnaise	250 mL
2	canned chipotle chile peppers in adobo sauce	2

1. In a food processor, pulse mayonnaise and chipotles with sauce until smooth. (If too thick, add water, 1 tbsp/15 mL at a time, until thinned to desired consistency.) Cover and refrigerate until chilled, about 20 minutes.

Jalapeño Mayonnaise

The intense flavor of pickled jalapeño peppers adds wonderful dimension to sandwiches. This mayonnaise is so easy to make, yet so tasty.

Makes about ½ cup (125 mL)

Tips

Store in an airtight container in the refrigerator for up to 1 week.

Spice up this recipe even more by adding a pinch or two of hot pepper flakes.

½ cup	mayonnaise	125 mL
3 tbsp	finely chopped drained pickled jalapeño pepper	45 mL
1 tbsp	grated lemon zest	15 mL
¼ tsp	salt	1 mL
¼ tsp	freshly ground black pepper	1 mL

1. In a bowl, combine mayonnaise, jalapeño, lemon zest, salt and pepper. Cover and refrigerate until chilled, about 20 minutes.

Horseradish Mayonnaise

This recipe is similar to Creamy Horseradish Sauce (page 243), but is thinner and has a slightly different flavor. Both work equally well as a spread for panini, but this one is a bit simpler.

Makes about 1 cup (250 mL)

Tips

Store in an airtight container in the refrigerator for up to 1 week.

For a bit more spice, add a pinch or two of freshly ground white pepper.

1 cup	mayonnaise	250 mL
2 tbsp	prepared horseradish	25 mL
2 tsp	freshly squeezed lemon juice	10 mL

1. In a bowl, combine mayonnaise, horseradish and lemon juice. Cover and refrigerate until chilled, about 20 minutes.

Wasabi Mayonnaise

I use this mayonnaise as a spread for seafood panini, especially those made with tuna or salmon. It's also great with sushi.

Makes about ½ cup (125 mL)

Tip
Store in an airtight container in the refrigerator for up to 1 week.

½ cup	mayonnaise	125 mL
2 tsp	prepared wasabi paste	10 mL
1 tsp	freshly squeezed lemon juice	5 mL

1. In a bowl, combine mayonnaise, wasabi paste and lemon juice. Cover and refrigerate until chilled, about 20 minutes.

Wasabi
Wasabi is found in both paste and powder forms at specialty and Asian markets, as well as some supermarkets. If you cannot find wasabi paste, substitute 2 tsp (10 mL) wasabi powder thinned with 3 to 4 tsp (15 to 20 mL) water. Stir into a paste and let stand for 5 to 10 minutes to release the flavor. If you're lucky enough to find fresh wasabi, grate it just as you would horseradish or gingerroot and add a very small amount at a time until the desired taste is achieved — be careful, it's fiery!

Quick and Easy Aïoli

Aïoli is basically garlic mayonnaise. It's served as an accompaniment to many dishes, both mains and sides. Classic aïoli is made with eggs and olive oil, but I've given you an easy version.

**Makes about
1 cup (250 mL)**

Tips

Store in an airtight container in the refrigerator for up to 1 week.

If you love garlic, feel free to add more!

5	cloves garlic	5
1 cup	mayonnaise	250 mL
¼ tsp	salt	1 mL
Pinch	freshly ground white pepper	Pinch
	Juice of ½ lemon	

1. In a food processor, pulse garlic, mayonnaise, salt, pepper and lemon juice until smooth. Cover and refrigerate until chilled, about 20 minutes.

Fay's Tartar Sauce

My mom made this sauce to accompany fried fish, shrimp or oysters. I loved it so much that I would have more tartar sauce on my plate than the entrée it should have complemented!

**Makes about
1 cup (250 mL)**

Tips

Store in an airtight container in the refrigerator for up to 1 week. Stir well before using.

For this recipe, you absolutely have to do the chopping by hand — a food processor won't give you the uniform pieces that are the key. If you're in a hurry, use dill pickle relish instead of chopping the pickle.

½ cup	finely chopped white or red onion	125 mL
½ cup	finely chopped dill pickle	125 mL
⅓ cup	mayonnaise	75 mL
½ tsp	freshly ground black pepper	2 mL

1. In a bowl, combine onion, pickle, mayonnaise and pepper. Cover and refrigerate until chilled, about 20 minutes.

Rémoulade

Rémoulade is great with fried seafood and with shrimp salads.

**Makes about
1½ cups (375 mL)**

Tips

Store in an airtight
container in the
refrigerator for up
to 1 week.

As this recipe chills,
the flavors marry and
mellow. I like to make
rémoulade the night
before I plan to use it.

2	cloves garlic, minced	2
1 cup	mayonnaise	250 mL
¼ cup	thinly sliced green onion	50 mL
2 tbsp	ketchup	25 mL
1 tbsp	chopped fresh parsley	15 mL
1 tbsp	spicy mustard	15 mL
1 tbsp	freshly squeezed lemon juice	15 mL
2 tsp	chopped drained capers	10 mL
1 tsp	paprika	5 mL

1. In a bowl, combine garlic, mayonnaise, green onion, ketchup, parsley, mustard, lemon juice, capers and paprika. Cover and refrigerate until chilled, about 20 minutes.

Classic Hollandaise

I learned this recipe when I was in culinary school at Johnson and Wales. I have never forgotten the technique, as I was a nervous wreck when I had to prepare hollandaise in front of the head chef as a test — but I passed! I use this sauce often, with many recipes.

**Makes about
¾ cup (175 mL)**

Tip

If your hollandaise
splits, whisk in a small
ice cube or ice-cold
water, 1 tbsp (15 mL)
at a time.

Double boiler

2	egg yolks	2
	Juice of ½ lemon	
½ cup	clarified butter, melted	125 mL
Pinch	salt	Pinch

1. In the top of a double boiler, whisk eggs. Gradually whisk in lemon juice. Place over simmering water (do not let boil). Add butter, 2 tbsp (25 mL) at a time, whisking until smooth. Add salt and cook, whisking constantly, until lemon yellow and thickened, 5 to 10 minutes. Serve immediately.

Olive Tapenade

I love olives, and the mix of flavors in this tapenade. Try it on sandwiches, as a dip, baked on crostini or tossed in pasta.

**Makes about
2 cups (500 mL)**

Tips

Store in an airtight container in the refrigerator for up to 2 weeks. Before serving, bring to room temperature and stir well.

This makes a great appetizer served with goat cheese and crackers or crusty bread.

I love Picholine olives, as they are mild and nutty. Sevillano olives, the most common green olives in the U.S., are often sold stuffed with pimientos.

Variation

A variety of herbs can be used in this recipe. According to your taste, add or substitute fresh basil, bay leaves, rosemary or marjoram.

1	anchovy fillet, drained and rinsed	1
1	clove garlic	1
1 cup	drained kalamata olives, pitted	250 mL
1 cup	drained green olives (such as Picholine or Sevillano), pitted	250 mL
1 tbsp	drained capers	15 mL
1 tbsp	chopped fresh Italian (flat-leaf) parsley	15 mL
1 tbsp	chopped fresh thyme	15 mL
1 tbsp	chopped fresh oregano	15 mL
1/4 tsp	hot pepper flakes	1 mL
1/4 cup	olive oil	50 mL
2 tbsp	freshly squeezed lemon juice	25 mL

1. In a food processor, pulse anchovy, garlic, kalamata and green olives, capers, parsley, thyme, oregano, hot pepper flakes, oil and lemon juice until chopped and somewhat smooth.

Tzatziki

This sauce is great with Greek salads, panini or gyros.

Makes about 2 cups (500 mL)

Tip

Store in an airtight container in the refrigerator for up to 3 days.

1 cup	shredded seeded peeled cucumber	250 mL
2	cloves garlic, minced	2
2	fresh mint leaves, finely minced	2
1 cup	plain yogurt	250 mL
1 tsp	white wine vinegar	5 mL
1 tsp	freshly squeezed lemon juice	5 mL
1 tsp	olive oil	5 mL
Pinch	salt	Pinch

1. Wrap cucumber in a paper towel and squeeze out excess liquid.

2. In a bowl, combine cucumber, garlic, mint, yogurt, vinegar, lemon juice, oil and salt, stirring well. Cover and refrigerate until chilled, about 20 minutes.

Creamy Horseradish Sauce

This recipe is always a favorite when served with wonderfully smoked prime rib, cooked to perfection — and beef panini recipes too!

Makes about 1½ cups (375 mL)

Tips

Store in an airtight container in the refrigerator for up to 1 week.

Lighten up this recipe by using low-fat sour cream, low-fat mayonnaise and half-and-half (10%) cream.

½ cup	sour cream	125 mL
½ cup	mayonnaise	125 mL
3 tbsp	whipping (35%) cream	45 mL
2 tbsp	prepared horseradish	25 mL
1 tsp	salt	5 mL
½ tsp	freshly ground white pepper	2 mL
½ tsp	granulated sugar	2 mL
	Juice of ½ lemon	

1. In a bowl, combine sour cream, mayonnaise, cream, horseradish, salt, pepper, sugar and lemon juice. Cover and refrigerate until chilled, about 20 minutes.

Cranberry Sauce

Although I love canned cranberry sauce, when I have time I like to make this homemade version, which is truly the easiest and the very best.

**Makes about
2½ cups (625 mL)**

Tip

Store in an airtight container in the refrigerator for up to 1 week. (Though it never lasts that long in my house!) Freshen up the flavor of the sauce by adding 1 tbsp (15 mL) freshly squeezed lemon juice before serving.

Variation

If you don't care for pecans, substitute raisins, currants or blueberries.

1 cup	granulated sugar	250 mL
1 tsp	grated orange zest	5 mL
1 cup	orange juice	250 mL
½ tsp	grated gingerroot	2 mL
1	package (12 oz/375 g) fresh or frozen cranberries	1
½ cup	chopped pecans, toasted (see tip, page 227)	125 mL

1. In a saucepan, combine sugar, orange zest, orange juice and ginger. Cook over medium heat, stirring, until sugar is dissolved, about 1 minute. Add cranberries and cook until they pop, about 5 minutes. Stir in pecans. Remove from heat and let cool.

Chipotle Barbecue Sauce

This sauce can be used in many ways. Here are a few ideas: slather it on pork or beef ribs right before taking them off the grill, drizzle it on sandwiches or use it as a sauce for chicken wings.

**Makes about
¹⁄₂ cup (125 mL)**

Tips

Store in an airtight container in the refrigerator for up to 1 month. Shake well before using.

The number of chipotle peppers you use will determine the spiciness of your sauce. If you want it super-spicy, use the adobo sauce as well.

1 to 2	canned chipotle chile peppers in adobo sauce, chopped	1 to 2
¹⁄₄ cup	ketchup	50 mL
1 tbsp	packed light brown sugar	15 mL
1 tbsp	light (white or golden) corn syrup	15 mL
1 tbsp	cider vinegar	15 mL
1 tbsp	Worcestershire sauce	15 mL

1. In a small saucepan, combine chipotles to taste, ketchup, brown sugar, corn syrup, vinegar and Worcestershire sauce. Cook over medium heat, stirring, until sugar is dissolved, 4 to 5 minutes.

Fresh Basil Pesto

This pesto is so fragrant, so fresh and so vibrant. You'll love it spread on panini or tossed with hot pasta.

**Makes about
1 cup (250 mL)**

Tip

Store in an airtight container in the refrigerator for up to 5 days. The oil will separate and float on top, which will help to preserve the rich green color. Stir before using.

1	clove garlic	1
3 tbsp	walnut pieces	45 mL
3 tbsp	pine nuts	45 mL
¹⁄₄ tsp	salt	1 mL
Pinch	freshly ground black pepper	Pinch
³⁄₄ cup	olive oil	175 mL
¹⁄₂ cup	freshly grated Parmesan cheese	125 mL
2 cups	packed fresh basil leaves	500 mL

1. In a food processor, pulse garlic, walnuts, pine nuts, salt and pepper until finely chopped. With the motor running, through the feed tube, gradually add oil in a slow, steady stream; process until combined. Add Parmesan and basil; pulse to combine, scraping down sides as needed.

Mushroom Pesto

This earthy pesto is wonderful smeared on panini, added to a cheese board or tossed with hot pasta.

Makes about 2 cups (500 mL)

Tips

Store in an airtight container in the refrigerator for up to 3 days. Stir before using.

Make bruschetta with mushroom pesto and freshly shaved Parmesan cheese.

4 tbsp	olive oil, divided	60 mL
10 oz	mushrooms, finely chopped	300 g
1 tbsp	Worcestershire sauce	15 mL
1 tbsp	dry white wine	15 mL
¼ tsp	salt	1 mL
¼ tsp	freshly ground black pepper	1 mL
1	clove garlic	1
¼ cup	pine nuts	50 mL
¼ cup	freshly grated Parmesan cheese	50 mL
½ cup	packed fresh parsley leaves	125 mL

1. In a skillet, heat 1 tbsp (15 mL) of the oil on medium-high heat. Add mushrooms, Worcestershire sauce, wine, salt and pepper; sauté until mushrooms are tender, about 5 minutes.

2. In a food processor, combine mushroom mixture, garlic, pine nuts and Parmesan. Add parsley and the remaining oil; pulse until combined and finely chopped.

Tomatillo Sauce

This authentic Mexican recipe is great on grilled meats, as a dip with tortilla chips or as a spread for panini or quesadillas.

Makes 2 to 3 cups (500 to 750 mL)

Tips

Store in an airtight container in the refrigerator for up to 2 weeks.

Add more garlic if you prefer a garlicky tomatillo sauce.

Anaheim peppers work especially well for roasting, so feel free to substitute them for the jalapeños.

Preheat oven to 425°F (220°C)
Roasting pan

1 lb	tomatillos, husked	500 g
4	jalapeño peppers, halved and seeded	4
4	cloves garlic	4
1	onion, quartered	1
½ cup	loosely packed fresh cilantro leaves	125 mL
2 tsp	ground cumin	10 mL
1 tsp	kosher salt	5 mL

1. In roasting pan, spread tomatillos, jalapeños, garlic and onion in a single layer. Bake in preheated oven until tomatillo and jalapeño skins are blistered and soft and garlic and onions are tender, 15 to 20 minutes. Let cool.

2. In a food processor, pulse roasted vegetables and juices, cilantro, cumin and salt until combined but still chunky. (If too thick, add water, 1 tbsp/15 mL at a time, until thinned to desired consistency.)

Black Bean and Corn Salsa

This salsa is so fresh and so versatile! You can serve it as a salad, as a dip or sandwiched between two flour tortillas, with a bit of Monterey Jack cheese, for the perfect quesadilla.

Makes 3½ to 4 cups (875 mL to 1 L)

Tips

Store in an airtight container in the refrigerator for up to 5 days.

To add more heat, use 2 jalapeños.

Roasted corn, cut right off the cob, will give this recipe a delicious charred flavor.

1	tomato, seeded and diced	1
1	jalapeño pepper, seeded and minced	1
1	can (14 to 19 oz/398 to 540 mL) black beans, drained and rinsed	1
1 cup	cooked fresh or frozen corn kernels, thawed if frozen	250 mL
¼ cup	thinly sliced green onion	50 mL
¼ cup	chopped fresh cilantro	50 mL
1 tbsp	freshly squeezed lime juice	15 mL
	Salt and freshly ground black pepper	

1. In a large bowl, combine tomato, jalapeño, beans, corn, green onion and cilantro. Add lime juice and toss to coat. Season to taste with salt and pepper. Cover and refrigerate until chilled, about 1 hour.

Caramelized Onions

I developed this recipe years ago but never wrote it down. I didn't need to — I use it so often, I know it by heart. But now it is time to share it, and I hope you enjoy it as much as I do. It makes a wonderful accent to many of the panini recipes in this book.

Makes about 1 cup (250 mL)

Tips

Store in an airtight container in the refrigerator for up to 1 week. Reheat in the microwave on High power for 45 to 60 seconds before using.

I like using red onions, but you can also use sweet white onions.

1 tbsp	olive oil	15 mL
1	red onion, thinly sliced	1
1 tbsp	packed brown sugar	15 mL
¼ tsp	salt	1 mL
¼ tsp	freshly ground black pepper	1 mL

1. In a large skillet, heat oil over medium-high heat. Add onion and sauté until softened, 10 to 15 minutes. Add brown sugar and cook, stirring gently, until onion is caramelized, about 5 minutes. Season with salt and pepper.

Perfect Guacamole

In 1993, my dear friend Bobby Collins got me hooked on guacamole; therefore, he is the inspiration for this recipe. As the title boasts, this guacamole is indeed perfect: perfect in panini, perfect with tortilla chips, perfect with salads, and especially perfect when a frozen margarita is served alongside!

Makes about 2 cups (500 mL)

Tips

For easier guacamole, substitute ½ cup (125 mL) of your favorite salsa or fresh pico de gallo for the tomatoes, jalapeños, garlic, red onion and cilantro.

I enjoy making and serving guacamole in a *molcajete*, the traditional Mexican version of a mortar and pestle.

2	large avocados, peeled and pitted	2
1 tbsp	sour cream, mayonnaise or ranch dressing	15 mL
3	plum (Roma) tomatoes, seeded and chopped	3
2	jalapeño peppers, seeded and minced	2
2	cloves garlic, minced	2
¼ cup	finely chopped red onion	50 mL
1 tbsp	chopped fresh cilantro	15 mL
2 tbsp	freshly squeezed lime juice	25 mL
	Salt and freshly ground black pepper	

1. In a bowl, roughly mash avocados. Stir in sour cream. Gently fold in tomatoes, jalapeños, garlic, onion, cilantro and lime juice. Season to taste with salt and pepper.

Library and Archives Canada Cataloguing in Publication

Collins, Tiffany
  200 best panini recipes / Tiffany Collins.

Includes index.
ISBN-13: 978-0-7788-0201-3.—ISBN-10: 0-7788-0201-9

  1. Panini. I. Title. II. Title: Two hundred best panini recipes.

TX818.C64 2008   641.8'4   C2008-902460-5

250

Index